Above

THE CITY

Above THE CITY

Hiking Hong Kong Island

Alicia M. Kershaw and Ginger Thrash

香港大學出版社
HONG KONG UNIVERSITY PRESS

Hong Kong University Press
14/F Hing Wai Centre
7 Tin Wan Praya Road
Aberdeen
Hong Kong

© Hong Kong University Press 2005

ISBN   962 209 736 7

Secure On-line Ordering
http://www.hkupress.org

British Library Cataloguing-in-Publication Data
A catalogue record for this book is available from the British Library.

Printed and bound by United League Graphic & Printing Co. Ltd., in Hong Kong, China

Contents

ACKNOWLEDGEMENTS

it is with all projects, many people help and contribute along the way.

So it is with us and we would like to take this time to thank those many friends
o helped us on this journey.

To Song Tharp, thanks so much for the many miles of companionship along the
ils, the constant support and the great idea of organizing the hikes around a hub!

Much appreciation goes to Jason Wordie for historical tips about Hong Kong place
mes. Knowing a bit about Lady Clementi adds a special charm to hiking her "ride."
 highly recommend Jason's *Streets: Exploring Hong Kong Island* (Hong Kong University
ss, 2003). Of course, we take responsibility for any errors in the information in this
ok.

Thanks to the many women in the American Women's Association and the YWCA
 hiking with us and giving us ideas and suggestions.

Before Colin Day agreed to take the book on, Doug Brown at Dairy Farm, Christina
ng and Lana Tsang at North Face, Charles Li and Derrick Young at Santa Fe Relocation
vices, and Paul Lucas at Home Front were willing to support this book with cold
rd cash. Their willingness to help is very much appreciated.

A huge thank you goes to Adriane Vasilikiotis, whose many hours of formatting
d graphics skills in the drafting stage of this book made us realize its visual potential.

Colin Day, our editor, spent hours getting us up a huge learning curve, with humor
d tact at all times, and also did a lot of footwork testing the routes. Phoebe Chan's eye
 detail and style is much appreciated. And a special note of thanks to Dick Yeung,
o translated our very roughly sketched maps into something not only readable but
ndsome.

And always, we must thank Peter and Jim for their ideas, patience and support
oughout this project. The hours of exploring new territory were wonderful adventures
d carrying that extra water was greatly appreciated.

And we would also like to thank each other, for a great friendship that survived —
leed thrived on — the writing of this book.

ABOUT THIS GUIDE

ng Kong Island offers some of the best and most accessible hiking trails we've tramped.
ew steps take you from the bustling city to a peaceful semi-tropical forest, full of
ds, and only a few less pleasant creatures. You can find hikes on Hong Kong Island to
t any mood — aerobic, leisurely, scenic, wooded, short, long, busy, or peaceful. (But
u won't find many flat ones!)

When we looked for information about Hong Kong's trails, we found that although
re are selective hiking guides available, a comprehensive guide to the trails did not
ist, so we wrote this one.

The hikes are grouped into five hubs, which are access points that are relatively
sy to find. Hikes are described from the hub. (In most cases the hike can also be done
reverse. If it is not obvious how to start at the end point, brief instructions are included
the end of the hike write-up.) Each hub includes a thumbnail sketch of every hike in
e hub.

The hub description has instructions for getting there on foot, by public transport
by car, and descriptions of nearby amenities, such as restaurants and toilets. Also,
ns representing different categories are there to help you decide what hike to choose
sed on factors such as: physically demanding, scenic, suitable for runners, children,
disabled people. Here is the key:

Fitness Trails
Disabled-Friendly Hikes
Kid-Friendly Hikes/Short Walks
Family Trails, Nature Walks, Tree Walks and Green Trails
Not-to-Be-Missed Hikes
Very Physically Demanding Hikes
Running Trails
Scenic/Historical Hikes
Morning Walkers' Gardens

e the appendices for the hikes grouped according to these factors.

As you walk along a trail, you will have many opportunities to veer from the m
path. The hike description identifies the options at each junction, so that you can des
your own hike. Variations and options are described at the point along the trail at wh
the option can be chosen, and the main route is listed first and in bold text. At the hi
end, we have included options for leaving the trail or continuing to hike. We have a
compiled a list of extended or combined hikes in the appendices.

Use this guide to plan your hike, then use it en route to keep you on the trail a
to make impromptu itinerary changes as you walk along. See you on the trail!

PES OF TRAILS

nage on trails in Hong Kong varies. Major trails are generally very well-marked, hough side paths and alternative routes may not be clearly indicated. The most popular ls have distance markers, as well as direction signs, usually providing the remaining tance and estimated walking time to the next trail point. Trails range from paved es to dirt tracks; many hill trails feature stairs made of concrete or stones.

We have noticed that the Hong Kong Government revises its trail signs from time time. When hiking paths, you may find, as we have, that the signposts we describe ve been changed slightly. Don't worry, the trails have not changed.

We've shown the estimated distance and time for each hike, based on government ns or maps. Government times are somewhat generous, but you soon learn how they mpare to your pace; and we have noted the few that seem substantially inaccurate. th time and distance shown are one way, and do not include time to return or get to from the hike. We've changed the format of the time listings to aid readability — tries like "1/12 hr" just seemed unnecessarily complicated when "5 min" would do.

Almost every trail in Hong Kong has hills — there just aren't many flat areas on the and! Each hike is ranked on a scale of 1 to 5 for difficulty (5 being most difficult). 've also included an estimate of "rise" for each trail — the height difference between e lowest and the highest points. (Note that hikes are ranked based on the route scribed — the return trip uphill will be much more difficult.) Difficulty is very bjective. We have tried to be consistent in ranking the hikes on our scale. We suggest u start with a few easier hikes to gauge how your personal scale relates to ours, before kling some of the harder hikes.

The Hong Kong Government has established two major trails on Hong Kong Island: e Hong Kong Trail (50 km) and the first two sections of Wilson Trail (78 km), which ntinues over to Kowloon via the MTR. Each Trail is divided into sections that require o 4 hours to hike; there is great variation among the sections. These two trails are remely well-marked and mapped, and at the beginning of each section signboards splay detailed maps.

The Hong Kong Parks Authority has established several trail types. "Family Trails," e easier routes, often dotted with educational markers identifying plant life. "Nature alks" and "Tree Walks," also designed for families, contain informational markers. reen Trails" contain markers with an environmental theme. "Fitness Trails" are fairly flat with exercise stations at various points along the way. "Morning Walke Gardens," small, peaceful garden paths, are tucked away off a couple of the main tra Country trails are longer routes laid out along a combination of trails, identified numerical markers preceded by C, i.e. C4109; other trails are noted with T marke i.e. T8112.

Since we wrote this guide, the Parks Department has begun posting maps combined hike routes, such as the Eastern District Nature Trail. Some of these can found at the Hong Kong government web site: http://www.afcd.gov.hk/parks/parks htm/; also see the "Extended Hikes" appendix for combined trails.

The Orienteering Association of Hong Kong has posted three courses, at Pok Lam Country Park, Aberdeen Country Park and Tai Tam Country Park (see Hikes 2E and 3C.) The Association can be reached as follows:

Telephone: 2504 8111
Fax: 2577 5595
Website: www.oahk.org.hk
E-mail: info@oahk.org.hk

MAPS

This guide includes fairly simple maps of the trails. In addition we use and recomme the Hong Kong Countryside Series Map, and have included cross references to its g in this guide. The black and white Government Trail Maps are also good. Both types available at the Government Bookstore, which can be reached through the Governmer "ESDlife" platform as follows:

Telephone hotline: 3151 2222

Website: http://bookstore.esdlife.com/eng/default.asp

The Countryside Maps are somewhat out of date and some side trails marked the maps have now disappeared into the overgrowth. We have included all trails that our experience can be relied upon to be clear.

WEATHER

In Hong Kong, you can hike all year long, although hiking is best in the fall and win (September to March). From April through August, be prepared for rain and hi humidity. May to November is typhoon season and hiking at that time of year can a be marred by torrential rain. Typhoon signals range from 1 (standby) to 10 (full fo gale). Don't hike if any signal has been hoisted. Rain warnings are Amber, Red a Black; all are too heavy for safe hiking, risking floods and landslides.

Most local TV stations display weather warnings.

Typhoon information: 2835 1473
Weather forecast: 187 8066
Hong Kong Observatory website: www.info.gov.hk/hko

COMMENDED EQUIPMENT FOR A HIKE

This guide.

Water — Take much more than you think you will need. Even in the cooler, drier season, Hong Kong's humidity dehydrates you very quickly.

Sun block, sun hat, sun glasses — The Hong Kong sun is very, very strong.

Insect repellent — Mosquitoes are your primary pest and lie in wait in wet areas.

Mobile phone — Some trails have emergency phones, which we have noted, but they are few and far between. If you are a tourist, you may want to rent a temporary phone through your hotel. Refer to the list of emergency numbers noted on the next page.

ID and medical alerts.

Maps — A compass could also be useful.

Walking stick — Helpful for your knees and also for dog and snake problems.

Toilet paper or tissues — Generally, Hong Kong toilets do not have toilet paper; you are expected to BYO. In most cases Hong Kong public toilets are clean; however, many of them do not have commodes. Some toilets are flushed with a bucket of water — in these cases you will find a large barrel of water in the toilet block. Used paper is deposited in a receptacle next to the toilet, not in the bowl/drain. Water in toilet blocks is NOT potable.

Sweatband and small towel — Helpful items to carry for hot and/or rainy weather.

Rain gear — It's often easier just to change clothes when you get home.

Flashlight — In case you get home later than you expected or need to use an unlighted toilet facility.

The following warnings need to be given but don't let them put you off. Hong ng is fun and safe to hike with a companion.

NOT HIKE ALONE

re are a few reasons why:

Slips and falls — In case of injury, you may need help.

Snakes — Yes, some are poisonous. We've only seen a few, in fact we've only seen their tails as any snake you get near will be doing its best to get away from you. Snakes are more commonly seen in the hotter months.

Wild dogs — A call to the Society for the Prevention of Cruelty to Animals won't help you here. Usually dogs are easily shooed away but they can be menacing.

IIs — Illegal immigrants. There have been a few recent incidents of IIs robbing hikers on Hong Kong Island, so be alert.

Flash floods — After rain, streambeds become flash flood zones. These areas are usually marked, and common sense should help you avoid danger.

- Mud slides — In the rainy season, slopes can become unstable and slip, which hazardous whether you are above or below the mud.
- Hornet nests — Be careful stepping off the trail as hornets make nests in the grou and will attack if stepped on.
- Hill Fires — Rarer on Hong Kong Island than on Lantau or in the New Territor In dry season the fire risk is monitored by the government and posted on signs the country parks.

STAY ON THE TRAIL

In many areas, the undergrowth surrounding the trail may disguise a sharp drop c Stay on ground you know is solid. If you take your dog: There have been several incide of dog poisoning in the Peak Area (Hub 1). Poisoned meats have been left on the tr. Keep your dog on a short leash, and if it eats anything left on the trail contact yo veterinarian immediately.

EMERGENCY NUMBERS

General Emergency: 999
Hill Fire Hotline: 999 or 2720 0777
Country Parks Info line: 2420 0529

GETTING THERE

Public transportation in Hong Kong is very easy to use, and we have indicated t appropriate bus and MTR stops for each Hub. The Octopus Card is a prepaid electron card used on the MTR and busses, and at some snack machines and shops. The card available in MTR stations and 7-Eleven shops. If you drive, you will need a prepa parking card for the meters. These are available at 7-Elevens. We have noted parki convenient to the hub, if it exists.

A brief word on types of public transport:

- Citybus and First World Bus — Drivers on main routes will know enough Engli to tell you when you have reached your stop, if you ask them to. On more remc routes the drivers may be less likely to speak much English, so take a map a point.
- Minibus/Maxicab — Yellow vans with green or red tops. You can flag these dov anywhere along their route and you can ask to be dropped off any where along t route. The driver may not speak much English, so take a map and point.
- MTR — The subway/MTR is very clean and quiet, though it can be crowde Announcements are made in English, Mandarin and Cantonese.

Taxis — Usually very reliable, but a map can be helpful. Taxis cannot pull over where double yellow lines are marked on the pavement; find a cab stand or an unmarked area on the street.

Happy trails! We hope this guide inspires you to get out and enjoy Hong Kong ʟing as much as we do.

VICTORIA GAP AT THE PEAK

Victoria Gap at the Peak is our number one hub for good reasons. It features numerous and varied walks, hikes, and running trails, many choices for a meal or refreshment, easy access, and fabulous views. There are also a few aggravations. Camera happy tourists, especially in groups, can impede a brisk walk or run; however, they don't often stray far from the Peak Tramway station. Local residents also take full advantage of the area, especially on weekends, taking constitutionals, walking with their families or practicing Tai Chi. Enjoy the popular hikes at less busy times or with a dose of patience, and save the aerobics for the less popular paths.

Map 1.1, 1.2, 1.3, 1.4

Countryside Map Grid: 06–07 and 65–66

To Get There

Bus:

Bus No. 15 from the Star Ferry runs every quarter of an hour and takes about one half hour. You can also pick it up in Wan Chai on Queen's Road East.

Tramway:

The Peak Tramway runs every 10 or 15 minutes from Garden Road (across from the U.S. Consulate, in the St. John's Building). The scenic ride on one of the oldest funiculars still in operation (built in 1888) is worth the fare.

Foot:

Old Peak Road from Tregunter Road or Conduit Road in Mid-levels; see Hike 1F

Conduit Road to Hatton Road; see the Morning Trail and Cheung Po Tsai Path; Hike 1B

Chatham Path and Central Green Trail from May Road; see Hike 1G

Pok Fu Lam Reservoir Road from Pok Fu Lam; see Hike 1J

Barker Road to Lloyd Path, Hospital Path or Findlay Path; see Hike 1H

Note: *Peak Road has no sidewalks and is not recommended for walking.*

Car:

Underground parking is available at the Galleria Building. There is limited metered street parking on Peak Road.

1A HONG KONG TRAIL SECTION 1 — THE PEAK TO POK FU LAM 🅝 🅡 🅢

The first section of the Hong Kong Trail affords spectacular views of both sides Hong Kong Island; each side has a completely different feel. Starting on Lugard Rc along the north side of the Island on paved roads that are easy to negotiate, but of crowded, the trail curves towards the south side, becoming a dirt path that follows contours of the canyons above Pok Fu Lam Reservoir. Much of this trail can be run

Distance: 7 km/4.4 mi	Difficulty: 2/5	Time: 2 hr
Rise: 200 m	Map 1.1	
Countryside Map Grid: • Start: 06–07 and 65–66 • Finish: 05–06 and 65		

1B THE MORNING TRAIL AND CHEUNG PO TSAI PATH 🅕 🅓 🅚 🅝 🅡 🅢

A pleasant walk from the Peak to Mid-levels, the Morning Trail has many attract features. First Harlech Road passes a flower filled waterfall and few, but striking, vie of the south side. Later, if you detour to the Pinewood Battery, a turn-of-the-cent defensive base, and the Lung Fu Shan Pavilion, there are excellent views to the we The section nearest the Peak Tramway Station includes fitness stations and is suita for jogging, if you don't mind dodging walkers and the occasional car. After High W Park, the trail heads steadily downhill, to the Cheung Po Tsai Path, a shady dirt tu named after a pirate. The path runs about a kilometer across the hill to a trail t returns you to the Peak.

Distance: 6 km/3.8 mi	Difficulty: 3/5	Time: 1 hr 30 min
Rise: 300 m	Map 1.1	
Countryside Map Grid: • Start and Finish: 06–07 and 65–66		
• Conduit Road: 05–06 and 66–67		

1C THE LOOP — HARLECH ROAD AND LUGARD ROAD (POK FU LAM TR WALK) 🅕 🅓 🅚 🅝 🅢 🅡 🅢

Combining Lugard Road (Hike 1A) and Harlech Road (Hike 1B), the Loop gi walkers and joggers a smooth paved path circling the Peak and beautiful views. It great walk and a good run: you have to decide how to tackle the incline on the no side — either the long more gradual rise, clockwise, or the shorter steeper way, coun clockwise. Or do it both ways! The views along the hill are worth a second look.

Distance: 3.5 km/2.2 mi	Difficulty: 2/5	Time: 1 hr
Rise: 70 m	Map 1.1	
Countryside Map Grid: • Start and Finish: 06–07 and 65–66		

1D GOVERNOR'S WALK AND VICTORIA PEAK GARDEN 🅚 🅢

Climb up to the top of Victoria Peak and enjoy the beautiful garden. This sh lk has just enough steps and incline to make it aerobic and the views are impressive. e garden features a pavilion on the site of the Mountain Lodge, the summer home of lonial Governors of Hong Kong for many decades. This hike can also be accessed m High West Park (Hike 1C or 1E) by a path up a short but steep series of stairs.

Distance: 1.1 km/0.7 mi	Difficulty: 2/5	Time: 30 min
Rise: 150 m	Map 1	
Countryside Map Grid: • Start and Finish: 06–07 and 65–66 • Victoria Peak: 05–06 and 66–67		

HIGH WEST (SAI KO SHAN) 🅢 🆇

High West is a very aerobic, very scenic, and very short hike that gives you a well-served sense of accomplishment. It starts at High West Park, then climbs directly up Ko Shan (494 m). Be prepared for stairs — about 200 of them. You must return wn the same route. Allow time to get to the park and back, along Lugard or Harlech ad or the Morning Trail, Hikes 1A, 1C, or 1B (15–45 mins.)

Distance: 0.4 km/0.25 mi	Difficulty: 3/5	Time: 15 min
Rise: 94 m	Map 1.1	
Countryside Map Grid: • Start and Finish: 05 and 65–66		

OLD PEAK ROAD 🅡

This pretty road, closed to through traffic until it crosses Tregunter Path, winds wnhill through dense foliage, and gives new meaning to the word steep. While lush h vegetation, it is not lush with views. It is a direct route to Mid-levels (at Robinson ad and the Botanic Gardens, see Countryside Map Grid 06–07 and 66–67). Old Peak ad can be combined with the Chatham Path and Central Green Trail (Hike 1G) or Morning Trail and Cheung Po Tsai Path (Hike 1B) to make a nice leafy loop.

Distance: 1.6 km/1 mi	Difficulty: 3/5	Time: 30 min
Rise: 220 m	Maps 1.2	
Countryside Map Grid: • Start: 06–07 and 65–66 • Finish: 06–07 and 66–67		

CHATHAM PATH AND CENTRAL GREEN TRAIL 🅚 🅝 🅡 🆇

The path is called a "Green Trail" because signs along the trail provide information out the plants and environment you see. Leafy and cool, it's pleasant, if not a lot to ite home about. If you want a good aerobic workout, do the hike in reverse, starting the Garden Road Peak Tramway Station and climbing up the Peak. A lovely shrine ng the way provides a good excuse to stop and catch your breath.

Distance: 2.75 km/1.7 mi	Difficulty: 2/5	Time: 45 min
Rise: 220 m	Map 1.2	
Countryside Map Grid: • Start: 06–07 and 65–66 • Finish: 07–08 and 66–67		

1H PEAK LOOPS 🅓 🅚 🅡 🆂

Several paths lead up, down or over the Peak and can be combined with each oth
or with the lightly traveled Peak back roads for enjoyable walks or runs. See Map 1.2 a
the detailed hike write-up for suggestions (Countryside Map Grid 06–08 and 64–66

1J POK FU LAM RESERVOIR FAMILY WALK 🅝 🅡

The Pok Fu Lam Reservoir Family Walk is a loop from the Peak to Pok Fu La
Reservoir Road and back. Rather challenging for a Family Walk (we can imagine
moaning if we took our kids), it's pretty and green but not terribly scenic. Half of t
loop is on Pok Fu Lam Reservoir Road, a wide paved path pitching steeply up hill; y
might consider doing the loop in reverse. It's good for running if you can handle t
steep incline.

Distance: 3.5 km/2.2 mi	Difficulty: 3/5	Time: 1 hr 30 min
Rise: 400 m	Map 1.3	
Countryside Map Grid: • Start and Finish: 06–07 and 65–66		
• Pok Fu Lam Reservoir Road ends at 04–05 and 65		

1K HONG KONG TRAIL SECTION 2 — POK FU LAM RESERVOIR ROAD TO PE RISE 🅕 🆂

Much of this section of the Hong Kong Trail is flat and wooded, but there are a
some long uphill pulls and steep steps down at the end. Bird's-eye views of Aberde
reward you at the end of the hike, about a 20-minute walk from Aberdeen.

Distance: 4.5 km/2.8 mi	Difficulty: 3/5	Time: 1 hr 30 min
Rise: 100 m	Maps 1.3	
Countryside Map Grid: • Start: 06–07 and 65–66 • Finish: 06–07 and 64		

1L HONG KONG TRAIL SECTION 3 — PEEL RISE TO WAN CHAI GAP 🅡

The trail is mostly flat and wanders under a canopy of trees, with a few interesti
views. It is suitable for running, or a cool walk on a hot day. At the end of the hike, y
must climb up steep Aberdeen Reservoir Road or Peel Rise to return to the Peak; s
Hike 1M.

Distance: 6.5 km/4 mi	Difficulty: 2/5	Time: 1 hr 45 min
Rise: 150 m	Maps 1.3	
Countryside Map Grid: • Start: 06–07 and 64 • Finish: 08 and 64		

1M PEEL RISE — THE PEAK TO ABERDEEN 🅡 🆂

You can get to Aberdeen from the Peak quickly on foot, and it's all downhill. Ta
Peel Rise from Peak Road and Mount Kellett Road, all the way to the center of Aberde

e road is steep, but has bountiful trees and a gurgling stream at the bottom.

Distance: 3.6 km/2.2 mi	Difficulty: 2/5	Time: 1 hr
Rise: 400 m	Maps 1.3	
Countryside Map Grid: • Start: 06–07 and 65–66 • Finish: 06–07 and 63–64		

MOUNT DAVIS TRAIL 🄺 🄡 🅂

A lesser-known hike, Mount Davis (269 m) offers fabulous views and a surprise at
e top. The trail is not directly accessible from the Peak, but it is on the west end of the
and (and it didn't fit in to any other Hub!). Start at Mount Davis Road and Pok Fu
m Road and complete the journey on Victoria Road.

Distance: 3.75 km/2.4 mi	Difficulty: 2/5 (road); 4/5 (stairs)	Time: 2 hr
Rise: 250 m	Map 1.4	
Countryside Map Grid: • Start and Finish: 03–04 and 66–67		

PIK SHAN PATH 🄡

A flat tree-shaded path good for running but not much else, although it does provide
ink to Mount Davis from Mid-levels and Pok Fu Lam. Pik Shan is a puzzle: only one
n labels the trail at all, and it says "To Pik Shan Pavilion" but neither Pik Shan nor its
vilion is labeled on our maps.

Distance: 3 km/1.9 mi	Difficulty: 1/5	Time: 30 min
Rise: negligible	Map 1.4	
Countryside Map Grid: • Start: 05–06 and 66–67 • Finish: 04–05 and 65–66		

⮡ *Hub Amenities*

e Peak has several restaurants and cafes, an ice cream shop and two grocery stores —
e Wellcome store is down Peak Road, not far from Mount Kellett Road. On Pok Fu
m Reservoir Road, near Pok Fu Lam, there is a vending machine for drinks at the
dy Maclehose P.H.A.B. Center. There is a tasty dim sum restaurant in Chi Fu Fa Yuen
ousing estate), as well as a grocery store, and small sidewalk stands on Pok Fu Lam
ad. In Aberdeen there are street side dai pai dongs (small shops selling cooked food).
 you can take a boat to the Jumbo Floating Restaurant, which is garish and touristy
t has good food and a fun atmosphere.

There are toilets located at the Peak Tramway Building, in the Galleria, at High
est Park and on Pok Fu Lam Reservoir Road at the reservoir.

Taxis and buses are plentiful on Pok Fu Lam Road and at Chi Fu, going to Aberdeen,
ntral and Stanley. Lines stopping at Pok Fu Lam Reservoir Road include Nos. 4, 7,
A, 40, 40M, 71, 91, 970, and 973.

Map 1.1   1A   1B   1C   1D   1E

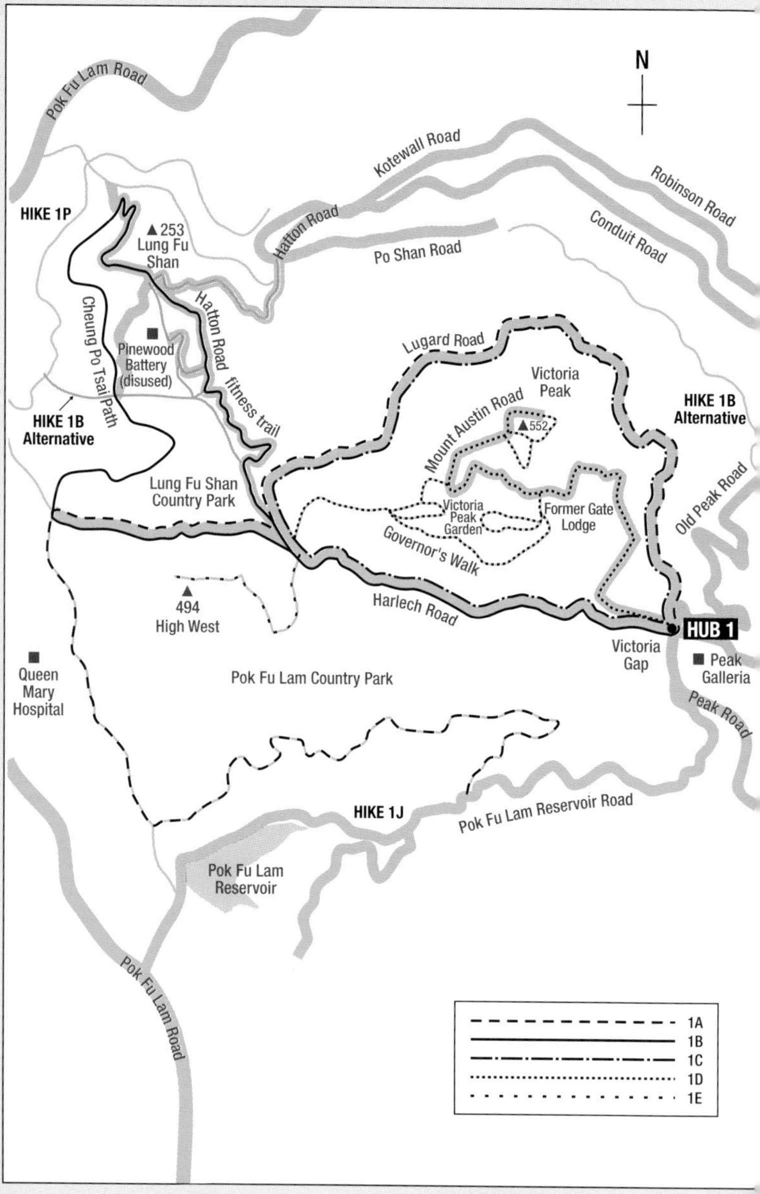

N

Pok Fu Lam Road

Kotewall Road

Robinson Road

Hatton Road

Conduit Road

HIKE 1P

▲ 253
Lung Fu
Shan

Po Shan Road

Cheung Po Tsai Path

Hatton Road fitness trail

Pinewood
Battery
(disused)

HIKE 1B
Alternative

Lung Fu Shan
Country Park

Lugard Road

Mount Austin Road

Victoria
Peak

▲ 552

HIKE 1B
Alternative

Victoria
Peak
Garden

Former Gate
Lodge

Governor's Walk

Old Peak Road

▲
494
High West

Harlech Road

HUB 1

Queen
Mary
Hospital

Pok Fu Lam Country Park

Victoria
Gap

■ Peak
Galleria

Peak Road

HIKE 1J

Pok Fu Lam Reservoir Road

Pok Fu Lam
Reservoir

Pok Fu Lam Road

– – – – –	1A
————	1B
–·–·–·–	1C
··········	1D
·–··–··–	1E

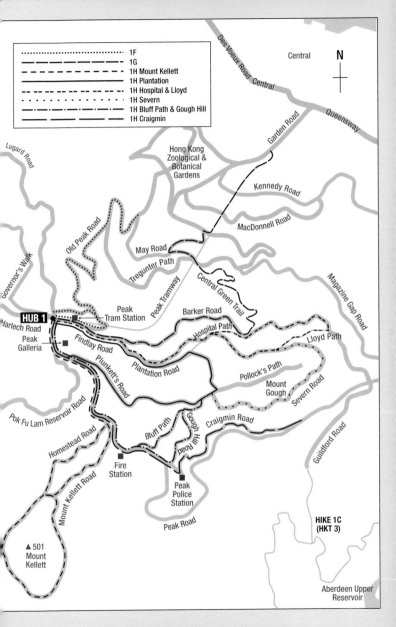

Legend:
- 1F
- 1G
- 1H Mount Kellett
- 1H Plantation
- 1H Hospital & Lloyd
- 1H Severn
- 1H Bluff Path & Gough Hill
- 1H Craigmin

Des Voeux Road Central

Central

N

Lugard Road

Hong Kong
Zoological &
Botanical
Gardens

Garden Road

Queensway

Kennedy Road

Old Peak Road

MacDonnell Road

Governor's Walk

May Road

Tregunter Path

Peak Tramway

Central Green Trail

Magazine Gap Road

HUB 1

Peak
Tram Station

Barker Road

Harlech Road

Peak
Galleria

Findlay Road

Hospital Path

Lloyd Path

Plunkett's Road

Plantation Road

Pollock's Path

Mount
Gough

Severn Road

Pok Fu Lam Reservoir Road

Bluff Path

Gough Hill Road

Craigmin Road

Guildford Road

Homestead Road

Fire
Station

Peak
Police
Station

Mount Kellett Road

HIKE 1C
(HKT 3)

Peak Road

▲ 501
Mount
Kellett

Aberdeen Upper
Reservoir

HIKE 1B

Lugard Road

▲ 552
Victoria
Peak

Victoria Peak
Garden

Old Peak Road

Peak
Tram Station

HIKE 1F

Tregunter Pa

The
Peak

HUB 1

▲ 494
High
West

Harlech Road

Victoria
Gap

Peak
Galleria

Pok Fu Lam Country Park

HIKE 1A

Family Walk

Pok Fu Lam Reservoir Road

Pok Fu Lam
Reservoir

paved lane

Mount
Kellett

Peel Rise

hacking trail (horse)

HIKE 1K
Alternatives

Pok Fu Lam
Gardens

Pok Fu Lam Reservoir Road

HKT 2

Pok Fu Lam Road

Hong Kong Trail

Peel Rise

Aberdeen Praya Road

Aberdee

Aberdeen West
Typhoon Shelter

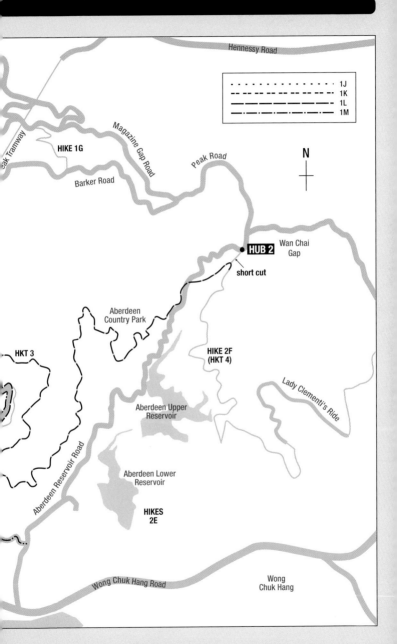

Hennessy Road

	1J
	1K
	1L
	1M

ak Tramway

HIKE 1G

Magazine Gap Road

Peak Road

Barker Road

N

HUB 2   Wan Chai
Gap

short cut

Aberdeen
Country Park

HKT 3

HIKE 2F
(HKT 4)

Lady Clementi's Ride

Aberdeen Upper
Reservoir

Aberdeen Reservoir Road

Aberdeen Lower
Reservoir

HIKES
2E

Wong Chuk Hang Road

Wong
Chuk Hang

N

Victoria Harbour

Sai Ying Pun

Des Voeux Road West

Kennedy Town

Belchers Street

Kotewall R

Victoria Road

stairs

Mount Davis Path

stairs

Youth Hostel

Mount Davis 269 ▲

Chiu Yuen Cemetery

overgrown trail

▲ 253 Lung Fu Shan

Po Shan Ro

HIKE 1B

Pinewood Battery (disused)

Hatton Road

Lugard Road

dead end

access road

reservoir

Mount Davis Road

Lung Fu Shan Country Park

Victo Pea

HKT 1

Harlech Road

Chinese Christian Cemetery

▲ 494 High West

HUE

reservoir

Victoria Road

HIKE 1A

HIKE 1J

Pok Fu Lam Road

Pok Fu Lam Reservoir Road

Pok Fu Lam Reservoir

Cyberport

················· 1N
—·—·—·—·—· 1P

10

A HONG KONG TRAIL SECTION 1 — THE PEAK TO POK FU LAM   Ⓝ Ⓡ Ⓢ

Ⓦe begin with the first section of the Hong Kong Trail, ⸢an⸣ excellent introduction to hiking in Hong Kong. The ⸢trai⸣l begins with fantastic views of Central Hong Kong ⸢and⸣ Victoria Harbor, stretching all the way to the New ⸢Ter⸣ritories; it then curls around the west end of the Island ⸢with⸣ views of Sulphur Channel and Lamma Island.

⸢Th⸣e first part of the trail (which is also Hike 1C) gradually ⸢slo⸣pes uphill as it winds its way around the Peak. It is ⸢pav⸣ed and wide enough for 2 or 3 people abreast. On ⸢we⸣ekdays you can see early morning walkers out for their ⸢Tai⸣ Chi exercises, some waving umbrellas or sticks, and ⸢peo⸣ple walking dogs. On the weekends the trail can be ⸢qui⸣te clogged with families and sight-seers. This part of ⸢the⸣ trail is also the Pok Fu Lam Tree Walk; signs identify ⸢tree⸣s along the path.

The second section is quite different; after you reach ⸢a sm⸣all pocket park, the trail becomes more rugged, with ⸢a d⸣irt and stone surface, and less open, with very few ⸢walk⸣ers. Small bridges cross rocky streams which flow ⸢abu⸣ndantly in the wet season. The hike ends near Pok Fu ⸢La⸣m Reservoir within Pok Fu Lam Country Park. Near ⸢the⸣ end, the trail is part of the Pok Fu Lam Reservoir Family ⸢Wa⸣lk, Hike 1J.

> Distance: 7 km/4.4 mi
> Difficulty: 2/5
> Time: 2 hr
> Rise: 200 m
> Ⓝ Map 1.1
> Countryside Map Grid:
> • Start: 06–07 and 65–66
> • Finish: 05–06 and 65

To Get There

⸢Th⸣e trail begins at the intersection at the west end of Peak Tramway Station. At the ⸢int⸣ersection, facing west, cross Peak Road and take a sharp right on Lugard Road. The ⸢Lu⸣gard Road sign is posted on the brick wall on the left, and the Hong Kong Trail sign ⸢a⸣ wooden sign posted on the right on a metal railing. There is also marker T8101.

Pause at marker H002 for one of the best views of the harbor, Central and Kowloon. ⸢Un⸣fortunately, there is no map board to help identify points of interest. Continue to ⸢lig⸣ht post 14615 and look down to the right on the hillside for the Turtle Rock, a large ⸢roc⸣k resembling a turtle adorned by a concrete cap. Pause again just before marker

11

H003. You will be directly above the Central Building. Facing west, look on the f
ridge for the old Pinewood Battery. The peak just beyond is Mount Davis (269 ▮
Little Green Island and Green Island are visible just off the tip of Hong Kong Isla
When we last went past, there was a bench on the right, just perfect for a rest stop
contemplate the view.

Along the flat path, mansions loom over you. On our last visit, one had a cage
birds, and near house No. 28 the tendrils of a beautiful *ficus elastica* tree hung over
The road slopes gradually upward and you pass a magnificent tree on the left; its rc
seem to be holding up the stone retaining wall.

After marker H005, the trail travels south to High West Park, with a playgrou
and fitness stations, and the intersection with Harlech Road. CHOICES:

- **Hong Kong Trail Section 1 — Turn right onto Hatton Road for a very sh
  distance, then go straight (do not go to the right down Hatton Road).**
- Morning Trail — Take the right fork (Hatton Road) a very short distance, th
  turn right, following the sign for the Morning Trail and Hatton Road — Hike
- Pok Fu Lam Reservoir via Harlech Road — 2 km/1.25 mi; 45 min — ahead
- Peak Tram Station — 1.25 km/0.8 mi; 15 min — ahead
- Peak Tram Station — 2.25 km/ 1.4 mi; 45 min — return to the Peak Tramv
  Station on Hong Kong Trail Section 1 and the Pok Fu Lam Tree Walk — back.

Other CHOICES include:

- High West (Sai Ko Shan) — Cross the Park and take the stairs (going down at fir
  at the southwest corner — Hike 1E.
- Governor's Walk — Take the short flight of steps on the left (uphill) just acr
  from the signpost — Hike 1D.

Note: There is a toilet a short distance down Hatton Road.

The path leads downhill about 1 km/0.6 mi then up a short flight of steps on
left to a rest area. There are picnic tables, many benches, and a good view, making t
a nice spot for a stop, but it is exposed with no shade. There is a location map t
identifies landscape features in the distance, including Lantau, Peng Chau, and Lam
Islands, and Kowloon. A signboard displays a map of Lung Fu Shan Country Park. T
signpost reads:

- **Pok Fu Lam Reservoir Road — 3.75 km/2.4 mi; 1 hr — ahead**
- The Peak Tram Terminus — 3.25 km/2 mi; 1 hr — back

Pick up the trail on the other side of the grassy area, just to the right of the me
rail fence, with stairs going down.

At marker H007 the trail drops down about 200 steps and is rather exposed. Qu▮

ry Hospital is directly in front of you. The view widens with Ebenezer School for the
ually Impaired directly in front as well the enormous Chinese Christian Cemetery.
the bottom of the series of stairs, take a sharp left turn, at the JUNCTION:

Pok Fu Lam Reservoir — 1.25 km/0.8 mi; 30 min — ahead (left)

Hatton Road — 1.5 km/0.9 mi; 30 min — right

The Peak via Lugard Road (Hong Kong Trail Section 1) — 3.75 km/2.4 mi; 1 hr
15 min — back

The path continues on dirt mixed with steps, fairly flat for the most part and with
 many views. Near marker H009 you abruptly arrive at an open area. Make a left
n, cross a concrete wall, and pass by a filter shed for the water treatment plant.
erlook the concrete for the view of the channel, with Lamma Island in the distance.
 soon arrive at a JUNCTION:

**The Peak via Pok Fu Lam Reservoir Road (Hong Kong Trail Section 1) —
3.75 km/2.4 mi; 1 hr 15 min — straight. At this point the trail is also the Pok Fu
Lam Family Walk; see Hike 1J.**

Chi Fu (a large housing estate, with amenities) — 3.5 km/2.2 mi; 1 hr 15 min —
straight

Pok Fu Lam Reservoir — 0.2 km/0.1 mi; 15 min — down steps to the right; see
Hike 1J

Peak Tram via Lugard Road — 4.5 km/2.8 mi; 1 hr 15 min — back

As you proceed, the trail contours the hillside, weaving in and out of the canyons.
 trail alternates between dirt and rock paving, following gentle rises and falls as it
sses many streams and stream beds. It is mostly flat with steps scattered throughout.

Many areas are tree covered; in more open areas, be sure to look up for views of
gh West (494 m), Victoria Peak (552 m), the Peak Tramway Station, and Mount
lett (501 m).

After you cross a large stream near marker H013, you will find a picnic site located
on the hill, but it might be intolerable in the mosquito season! Follow the flat shaded
h, which will suddenly drop down very steep stairs, and immediately turn right back
 again. Antler ferns adorn the hill.

Hong Kong Trail Section 1 ends just beyond marker H014 on Pok Fu Lam Reservoir
ad. A short distance down the road two sets of markers lay out your CHOICES:

Hong Kong Trail Section 2 — Peel Rise — 4.7 km/2.9 mi; 1 hr 30 min — down the
road a short way and then left — Hike 1L

Pok Fu Lam Reservoir Family Walk — down the road to the gate — Hike 1J

Peak Tramway Station via Lugard Road — 6.8 km/4.2 mi; 1 hr 50 min — back

For a quicker return to the Peak, follow the sign pointing up Pok Fu Lam Reservoir
Road to the left — 1.3 km/0.8 mi; 30 min.

To Leave the Trail

- Chi Fu [Housing Estate] — 1.6 km/1 mi — down the road a short way and t█ left

- Pok Fu Lam Road via Pok Fu Lam Reservoir Road — 1.1 km/0.7 mi; 15 min — the right and down; see Hike 1J

B THE MORNING TRAIL AND CHEUNG PO TSAI PATH

𝕱 𝔻 𝕂 ℕ ℝ 𝕊

popular choice, the Morning Trail and Cheung Po
Path route combines beautiful views and many fitness
ions. You can walk or run the first part, stopping to
np iron and enjoy the south side views at the fitness
ions. Then, as you trot down the north side of Mount
stin towards Mid-levels on Hatton Road, you can stop
the Pinewood Battery and the Lung Fu Pavilion, both
e remarkable views. After asking the blessing of a
ldha mounted on a slope, you can cross Lung Fu Shan
the Cheung Po Tsai Trail, said to be a pirate's lookout,
return to the Peak along its southern flank. If you
er, you can end your hike in Mid-levels.

> Distance: 6 km/3.8 mi
> Difficulty: 3/5
> Time: 1 hr 30 min (loop)
> Rise: 300 m
> 🧭 Map 1.1
> Countryside Map Grid:
> • Start and Finish:
>   06–07 and 65–66
> • Conduit Road:
>   05–06 and 66–67

To Get There

trail begins at the intersection at the west end of the Peak Tramway Station.
he intersection, facing west, cross Peak Road and proceed straight ahead along
flat Harlech Road, signed the Morning Trail (2,800 m). The Morning Trail has
rkers every 100 meters.

Enjoy the beautiful waterfall at 200 meters, and then look for views to the south. If
trail has not been trimmed recently you may have to peer through some shrubbery,
you will be able to see Pok Fu Lam and the Pok Fu Lam Reservoir, with Lamma
nd in the distance.

Between 500 and 700 meters there are fitness stations such as "Sit Up," "Spring
" and "Pull Up Bars." **There is an emergency phone near the 900-meter marker.**

High West Park, at 1,100 meters, is enjoyed by exercisers, dog walkers, school
ldren, Tai Chi enthusiasts and morning hikers. It contains picnic sites and more
ess areas. The park is the focal point for several CHOICES:

**Morning Trail — Take the left fork a very short distance, then turn right,
following the sign for the Morning Trail and Hatton Road following the sign
for Pok Fu Lam Reservoir via Harlech Road — 2 km/1.25 mi; 45 min — back**
Peak Tram Station — 2.25 km/1.4 mi; 45 min — Return to the Peak Tramway
Station on Hong Kong Trail Section 1 and the Pok Fu Lam Tree Walk (on Lugard
Road) — Hike 1C.
Peak Tram Station — 1.25 km/0.8 mi; 15 min — back (note discrepancy in distance
compared to 1,100-meter marker)

Other CHOICES include:

- High West (Sai Ko Shan) — Cross the park and take the stairs (going down at fi
at the southwest corner — Hike 1E.
- Governor's Walk — Take the short flight of steps on the right (uphill) just acr
from the signpost — Hike 1D.
- Hong Kong Trail Section 1 — Follow the Morning Trail onto Hatton Road f
very short distance, then go straight (do not go to the right down Hatton Road)
Hike 1A.

On the left a sign says "Morning Trail Hatton Road — right; Morning Trail Harl
Road — back," and down the path you do not take you see a BBQ sign, a Tree Walk s
and a Hong Kong Trail marker. Another sign directs you right to Hatton Road. You p
a map board, toilets, a sign for Lung Fu Shan Country Park ("Hill Above Belcher
(253 m), and a JUNCTION marker:

- **Pinewood Battery — ahead**
- Kotewall Road — 2 km/1.25 mi; 45 min — ahead. Kotewall Road intersects w
Conduit and University Drive at the end of Hatton Road.
- Pokfield Road — 2 km/1.25 mi; 45 min — ahead. Pokfield Road leads to Kenn
Town off Pok Fu Lam Road, some distance from the end of Hatton Road.
Countryside Map Grid 04–05 and 66–67.
- The Peak — 1.25 km/0.8 mi; 30 min — back

A distance marker shows you have come 1,200 meters and have 1,600 meter
the end of the Morning Trail.

The next 200 meters are part of the Lung Fu Shan Fitness Trail, starting wi
waist tape measure and body mass index chart. The trail includes foot massage be
parallel bars, leg stretches and "step rocks," as well as exercise tips.

Wind steadily down the hill on Hatton Road in and out under a canopy of trees
1,400/1,400 meters, steps lead down to the turn of the century Pinewood Battery.
battery was completed in 1905 but declared superfluous in 1907 in a cost cutting m
then reactivated in the 1930s. It was attacked by the Japanese on 15 December 19
then abandoned. You have three chances on the way down to detour there, and we a
describe a way to visit on the way back up. This option takes you down about 250 st
to the battery.

At 1,800/1,000 meters, steps uphill on the left again lead to the battery; howe
if you **press on to just before 1,900/900 meters**, a short detour to the left also le
there. At this JUNCTION:

- **Pokfield Road — 1.25 km/0.8 mi; 15 min — or Kotewall Road — 1 km/0.6
30 min — ahead**

The Peak — 2 km/1.25 mi; 45 min — back
Pinewood Battery and BBQ sites — left

Back on the trail, pass unmarked steps on the left to the battery, then continue
ᵥn along an open section with a very nice view over Yau Ma Tei, to a 2,200/600-
ter marker, and a JUNCTION:

Pokfield Road — 1 km/0.6 mi; 15 min — left
Morning Trail — straight ahead (Hatton Road)
Pinewood Battery — back, or up stairs to the left of Pokfield Road
Lung Fu Shan Pavilion — a side trip well worth the effort for the views — left
Kotewall Road — 0.75 km/0.5 mi; 15 min — ahead
The Peak — 2.25 km/1.4 mi; 1 hr — back

ᵤnt a small rise to a JUNCTION:

Pokfield Road — 1 km/0.6 mi; 15 min — and Planting Site Number 2 — right
Planting Site Number 1 — left
Kotewall Road — 0.75 km/0.5 mi; 15 min — back
The Peak — 2.25 km/1.4 mi; 1 hr — back
Pok Fu Lam Reservoir — 2.75 km/1.7 mi; 1 hr — left

The Planting Sites are garden plots, with plants and shrubs labeled (in Chinese).
ᵏing the paved lane to the right, you pass a toilet on the right and stairs (over 100) up
ᵗhe Lung Fu Shan Pavilion — it's worth it!
Look for a colorful frieze of the dragon and phoenix, followed by a frieze of the
ᵢitreya Buddha, on the slopes on the right. Walk down the road, steep in parts, past a
ᵗh down to Planting Site Number 2, and several viewing pavilions. There are not
ᵢny views from the road, but the views from the pavilions are delightful — you can
ₑ the Tsing Yi Bridge and the container port.
A few turns down the hill there is another sign for Planting Site Number 2, with
ᵢrs down to the left. (A dirt trail a bit further along is a short cut to the trail.) Four
ᵢtch backs later, you come to a JUNCTION:

Planting Site Number 1 — take the stairs then turn left on the dirt trail.
Pokfield Road — 0.5 km/0.3 mi; 15 min — ahead
to leave the trail here see Alternatives

You are now on the Cheung Po Tsai Path, rumored to be the look-out trail of infamous pirate who bedeviled the Emperor in pre-colonial days. The name may be apocryphal, as there are very few views. However, the views you do get are remarka Cheung could have seen ships coming down from the Pearl River Delta, and he co also have kept watch on Cheung Chau Island, rumored to be his hideout. The p crosses the hillside for about a kilometer through a pretty forest. At the end, a few st lead to the north end of a paved road. This road begins at the junction off Hatton R (where we took a right turn to Pokfield Road at the Lung Fu Shan Pavilion). A s reads:

- **Planting Site Number 1 — ahead**
- Pokfield Road — 1.5 km/0.9 mi; 30 min — back

Turn right on the road. Benches line the road, as well as "hangers," which are ra with clothes pegs for Tai Chi enthusiasts to use when they work up a sweat and nee shed a layer or two. At pavilion at the end, the sign reads:

- Planting Site Number 1 — ahead
- Hatton Road — 0.5 km/0.3 mi; 15 min — back

There is a toilet, **an emergency phone** and stairs down, and up to the left a s that reads:

- **Pok Fu Lam Reservoir (Family Tree Walk) — 2.25 km/1.4 mi; 45 min — ahe**
- Planting Site Number 1 — ahead and down — about 300 steps down pass Planting Site and end up on Pok Fu Lam Road at Y. Y. Mansions, No. 94. The st cross the Pik Shan Trail, Hike 1P.
- Hatton Road — back
- Pinewood Battery and BBQ site — 0.25 km/0.1 mi; 15 min — left

The path marked "Pok Fu Lam Reservoir" climbs slowly with a mix of steps a dirt along a very pretty stream bed, with few views, but as you climb higher, on m and more steps, you begin to get very fine views out to Green Island and looking b to Tsing Yi. You start out with a few short warm-up flights of steps, mixed with sections, then hit a long 100 or so step rise, peaking at a marker overlooking Que Mary Hospital and a JUNCTION:

- **The Peak via Lugard Road (Hong Kong Trail Section 1) — 3.75 km/2.4 1 hr 15 min — left — Hike 1A**
- Pok Fu Lam Reservoir (Hong Kong Trail Section 1) — 1.25 km/0.8 mi; 30 min ahead — Hike 1A
- Hatton Road — 1.5 km/0.9 mi; 30 min — back (note time difference from the s of the road, which says 15 min)

From here, climb up past Hong Kong Trail marker H007 and onto the paved path ck up to the Peak, ending at High West Park; see Hike 1A.

Alternatives

Above the pavilion at Planting Site Number 1, the steps marked "Pinewood Battery and BBQ site" are another way back up to the Peak, passing a frieze of a reclining Buddha on the way. Two hundred seventy steps later, when the path becomes a dirt trail, stop and rest, and turn around for a clear, long view. After a brief respite of short flights of stairs intermixed with flat sections, climb about 70 more steps to a BBQ area, just above the Pinewood Battery. The JUNCTION says:

The Peak (via Lugard Road) — 3.25 km/2 mi; 1 hr 15 min — right — about 250 steps to the 1,400/1,400–meter marker on Hatton Road

Pinewood Battery — left

Morning Trail/Hatton Road — unmarked, the path straight ahead meets the road just above the 1,900/900-meter marker — turn right on the road to return to the Peak.

Pok Fu Lam Reservoir — 2.5 km/1.6 mi; 1 hr — back — rather odd signage as it takes you away from the reservoir, but it does eventually connect to the trail to the reservoir, described above.

A marker to the right indicates the Lung Fu Shan Fitness Trail to the right, a route at also returns you to the Peak.

Instead of Cheung Po Tsai Path you could take the Pik Shan Path to cross the hillside. You can pick up Pik Shan Path at the end of Hatton Road or by following the Pokfield Road signs. See Hike 1P.

To leave the trail before starting along Cheung Po Tsai Path, stay on the lane at the JUNCTION after you pass Planting Site Number 1.

After passing a viewing pavilion on the left, it fades into a trail, with steps down, at a sign reading:

- Pokfield Rd — 0.5 km/0.3 mi; 15 min — back

The path crosses the Pik Shan Trail, Hike 1P, at a sign:

- Pokfield Road — down
- Hatton Road/Pinewood Battery — up

Continuing down, the trail becomes a stone path with even, comfortably spac[ed] steps down. After 35 steps, more or less (somehow it always seems like more, [not] less), and then about 300 concrete stairs down, past a pavilion, you arrive at [the] gas station on Pok Fu Lam Road at Pokfield Road. See Countryside Map Grid [0]5 and 66–67. Find this trail at the hydrant by the petrol station. Other exits [are] described in Hike 1P.

4. You can shorten your hike a bit, and make it more comfortable for running, [by] taking a left at the first signs for Planting Site Number 1 and 2. Hangers and benc[hes] dot the roadside, and there are nice, if sparse, views over to the west. There is ev[en] a pavilion with smooth stones laid in a bed of concrete for foot massages. Trend[ing] downhill, pass a bridge with railings over a runoff channel, then a pavilion and [to] its right, the marker for Cheung Po Tsai's Path (which reads "Pokfield Road[). Keep going past more hangers and benches to the end of the road, then take [a] left to the Peak, indicated by the sign "Pok Fu Lam Reservoir (Family T[rail] Walk)" — 2.25 km/1.4 mi; 15 min.

5. Cheung Po Tsai Path extends from the starting point we describe above back [to] Hatton Road, but it is so overgrown it has been signed "off limits" by [the] Government. If you take a machete, and perhaps a large dog, you might try it. T[he] path starts just before the end of the road to Pokfield Road, at a pavement cut o[ut] marked by a "Road Closed" sign. It ends on Hatton Road across from the Sitti[ng] Out Area at light pole No. 41688. The path once ran to Po Shan Road but is t[oo] overgrown to locate.

6. If you prefer to take the Morning Trail to its end, about a 45-minute walk over[all] follow it down, passing a Lung Fu Shan Country Park sign and one of many sig[ns] in the park commemorating a morning walkers' club. Arriving at 2,400 mete[rs] you are rewarded with a bench and an old City Boundary marker, dated 1903, [on] the right side of the road. Also on the left a bit further down is yet another sign [for] the Lung Fu Shan Fitness Trail, which probably means the government really wa[nts] you to work out! The Fitness Trail emerges on Hatton Road around marker 1,4[00?] 1,400 meters. Another 200 meters brings you to the Hatton Road Sitting Out Ar[ea]. All too soon you pass the Fire Station on the left, cross over Po Shan Road on [an] overpass (you can take the stairs to the left, down to the road, and pick up [a] minibus to the Star Ferry), and merge into the intersection of Hatton, Kotewa[ll] and Conduit Roads in Mid-levels. See Countryside Map Grid 05–06 and 66–67[.]

From here, turn right along Conduit Road to Robinson Road to pick up C[?] Peak Road (Hike 1F) or the Chatham Path and Central Green Trail (Hike 1G).

There is, however, a path of sorts from Po Shan Road to Old Peak Road, if it has not become too overgrown. As Po Shan turns downhill and narrows, look for a few steps down to the right. We can't say it has much to recommend it, as it is weedy and surrounded by chain-link fences but it is there, and fine for running.

Or, to leave the trail, take bus No. 13 to the Star Ferry or walk along Conduit Road to reach the escalator down through Mid-levels and into Central, with plenty of places to replenish your energy. You can also take minibus 3 or 3A to Central.

e: *The escalator runs downhill only from 6:00 a.m. to 10:00 a.m.; at other times, you must take the stairs alongside.*

1C THE LOOP — HARLECH ROAD AND LUGARD ROAD (POK FU LAM TREE WALK)

F D K N S R X

A rarity for hikes in Hong Kong, this trail is both flat (for the most part) and very scenic — but you can't avoid a good-sized hill on the north side! A versatile choice, you can jog, run, walk, try your hand at the fitness course, and combine it with any number of other hikes. The views are among the best and include both the north and south sides of the Island. This is the perfect walk to show off Hong Kong to visiting friends and family.

> Distance: 3.5 km/2.2 mi
> Difficulty: 2/5
> Time: 1 hr
> Rise: 70 m
> Map 1.1
> Countryside Map Grid:
> • Start and Finish:
>   06–07 and 65–66

To Get There

The loop combines Hikes 1A and 1B, starting with 1B.

The trail begins at the intersection at the west end of the Peak Tramway Station. the intersection, facing west, cross Peak Road and proceed straight ahead along the Harlech Road, signed the Morning Trail (2,800 m). The Morning Trail has mark every 100 meters.

Enjoy the beautiful waterfall at 200 meters, and then look for views to the south the trail has not been trimmed recently you may have to peer through some shrubbe but you will be able to see Pok Fu Lam and Pok Fu Lam Reservoir, with Lamma Isla in the distance.

Between 500 and 700 meters there are fitness stations, "Sit Up," "Spring Up" a "Pull Up Bars." **There is an emergency phone near the 900-meter marker.**

High West Park, at 1,100 meters, is enjoyed by exercisers, dog walkers, sch children, Tai Chi enthusiasts and morning hikers. It contains picnic sites and m fitness areas. The park is the focal point for several CHOICES:

- **The Loop — bear right on Lugard Road — 2.25 km/ 1.4 mi; 45 min — sign "Peak Tram Station"**
- Pok Fu Lam Reservoir via Harlech Road — 2 km/1.25 mi; 45 min — back
- Peak Tram Station — 1.25 km/0.75 mi; 15 min — back

Other CHOICES include:
- Morning Trail — Take the left fork a very short distance, then turn right, follow the sign for the Morning Trail and Hatton Road — Hike 1B.

High West (Sai Ko Shan) — Cross the park and take the stairs (going down at first) at the southwest corner — Hike 1E.

Governor's Walk — Take the short flight of steps on the right (uphill) just across from the signpost — Hike 1D.

Hong Kong Trail Section 1 — Follow the Morning Trail onto Hatton Road for a very short distance, then go straight (do not go to the right down Hatton Road) — Hike 1A.

At this point, you will be on the first part of the Hong Kong Trail Section 1 (in erse), which is also the Pok Fu Lam Tree Walk.

Along the flat path, mansions loom over you. On our last visit, one had a cage of ds, and near house No. 28 the tendrils of a beautiful *ficus elastica* tree hung over us. e road slopes gradually upwards and you pass a magnificent tree on the right; its ts seem to be holding up the stone retaining wall. Pause at markers H002 and H003 ake in some of the best views of Hong Kong: the harbor, Mid-levels, Central, Kowloon on a clear day, you can see forever (well, to China, which is quite far enough!) After rker H003, at light post 14615 look down to the left on the hillside for the Turtle ck, a large rock resembling a turtle adorned by a concrete cap.

Continue along as the road eases back down, past a few more mansions, to the rt.

To Continue to Hike

Old Peak Road — Hike 1F

Peak Loops — Hike 1H

Pok Fu Lam Reservoir Family Walk — Hike 1J

Hong Kong Trail Sections 2 or 3 — Hike 1K or 1L

Peel Rise — the Peak to Aberdeen — Hike 1M

Alternatives

r an even better work out, start at Mid-levels or Central (see Hub 1, "To Get There," n Foot").

1D GOVERNOR'S WALK AND VICTORIA PEAK GARDEN

This short scenic trail, tucked away at the top of Victoria Peak (552 m), treats you to a bonus: the lovely Victoria Peak Garden. The main part of the trail alternates flat sections with stairs around the south side of Mount Austin, parallel to but above Harlech Road; the rest twines through the garden, which is fun to explore. The trail is topped off by a large Pavilion, situated just right for enjoying the terrific views, on the site of Mountain Lodge, the summer residence for colonial Governors from 1867 to the Second World War.

Distance: 1.1 km/0.7 mi
Difficulty: 2/5
Time: 30 min
Rise: 150 m
Map 1.1
Countryside Map Grid:
• Start and Finish:
  06–07 and 65–66
• Victoria Peak:
  05–06 and 66–67

To Get There

The trail begins at the intersection at the west end of the Peak Tramway Station. At intersection, facing west, cross Peak Road and take Mount Austin Road, which ru uphill between the two flat roads (Lugard and Harlech Roads).

Follow Mount Austin Road to the top, passing Mount Austin Playground, seve apartment complexes and the Mount Austin Rest Garden. At the only junction there a sign on the curb that directs you straight ahead to Victoria Peak Garden. Soon y will come to a small house on the left, which is used by the park gardeners now but w previously the gatehouse for the Governor's summer residence.

CHOICES:
• **Pass the gatehouse and take the signed stairs down to the left.**
• Walk up Mount Austin Road to the pavilion.

You pass above a large open field on the right; many people come here to sit on benches, let their dogs romp and enjoy the space. The trail quickly comes to a JUNCTIO with a sign indicating Governor's Walk to both the left and right:
• **Governor's Walk — left**
• Directly up to the pavilion through the garden — right. You will visit it later in hike.

Pass a pretty little stream. The path narrows and immediately opens up to reveal nd vistas to the east. As you round the hill, the views move to the south, including ɪma Island and Mount Kellett (501 m) as well as back to the Peak Tramway Station. ɪch where you place your feet; the trail drops off sharply to one side.

The path travels down and up with steps sprinkled throughout, and traverses a ᴘle of flat sections. Here there are no views, as the shrubs and trees are quite high ɪ this short section is very shady. Soon the trail once again becomes flat and more ɪn, with brief views of nearby High West (494 m).

At light post No. 47 there is a JUNCTION:

Continue — sharp right up the steep slope

To exit the trail or access High West (Hike 1E), the Morning Trail (Hike 1B), Hong Kong Trail Section 1 (Hike 1A), or the Loop (Hike 1C) — left, along a trail that gradually slopes down with many stairs to High West Park (about 0.4 km/ 0.25 mi).

Look back occasionally to see High West and Cheung Chau Island in the distance. At light post No. 51, another JUNCTION:

To reach the large covered pavilion — left, up the stairs.

To reach a large grassy area and some welcome benches — straight.

The views are some of the best in Hong Kong and made more enjoyable by the ɒling breeze that is almost always wafting by. As well as the pavilion, there is a small ᴡing area set off to the west along a short path. There are benches to sit on as you ɪk out over the channel. When you are ready to leave, you have two CHOICES:

Back to the gatehouse via Mount Austin Road.

Down the stairs across from the parking lot, turn left to the path that re-connects with Mount Austin Road.

Alternatives

ɒnnect with Governor's Walk from High West Park. To get there, take Harlech Road or ɡard Road from the Peak (see Hike 1C) or Hatton Road from Mid-levels (see Hike ᴅ) to High West Park, and go up the stone stairs into the trees, across from the signpost ɪhe park. You will meet the Governor's Walk at light post No. 47; see above.

Amenities

ᴜ weekends, a refreshment stand is open at the Garden Pavilion.

1E HIGH WEST (SAI KO SHAN) 🇸 🇽

Appropriately named, High West (494 m) offers panoramic views of the west end of the Island, with maps at the top to help you find the landmarks. You can see all the way to Cheung Chau Island in the west and the islands in the harbor to the east. Of course, you will have to work a bit for the reward, but it is definitely worth the effort to get there. Get your knees ready for lots of stairs. Short and sweet, High West makes a great addition to any of the hikes around the Peak Hub. Time and distance shown are one way.

Distance:
- 0.4 km/0.25 mi from High West Park
Difficulty: 3/5
Time: 15 min
Rise: 94 m
🇳 Map 1.1
Countryside Map Grid:
- Start and Finish: 05 and 65–66

To Get There

The trail starts at High West Park. At the intersection at the west end of the Peak Tramw Station, take either Lugard Road (sharp right) or Harlech Road (flat road straight ahe to High West Park. Harlech is the shorter route (1.25 km/15 min vs. 2.25 km/45 mi

As you face High West Park (facing west), walk down the few steps into the P and go to the far southwest corner (past the parallel bars and the vault bars). Take short flight of stairs going down to the left (south) and then follow the tree lined stepp stone pathway. Shortly, the trail passes between two concrete structures and th suddenly arrives at an open area. There is a nice, secluded table with benches on top the larger structure.

For now, keep this spot in mind for a break on your return. Cross the open gr area. High West is on your right, clearly showing the work cut out for you. The trai all steps. You might find a lizard or two basking in the sun and kites (native haw soaring on the heat waves, searching for a meal. At the top of the hill, cross a sh ridge, and then go up just a few more stairs to the look out and superb views. M have been posted, identifying the landmarks in view.

Return the way you came, stopping at the picnic area to snack or rest if you wi

Alternatives

If the stairs are too daunting, one alternative is the pocket park on the Hong Kong Tr just below High West. It too has views and benches. At High West Park, follow the si for Hong Kong Trail Section 1. It's just 1 km/0.6 mi down the gently sloping path to park. See Hike 1A.

F OLD PEAK ROAD

R

ld Peak Road doesn't offer much in the way of views,
it is one of our favorite short workout hikes. The trail
ers verdant forest and gushing streams. You will have a
l sense of accomplishment when you have finished,
ecially if you take it in reverse. The trail can be added
many of the Peak Hub hikes to make good loops. The
od news: the road switchbacks down the hill (all but
known in Hong Kong trails). The bad news: it is so
ep that your knees and thighs will moan.

Distance: 1.6 km/1 mi
Difficulty: 3/5
Time: 30 min
Rise: 220 m
N Map 1.2
Countryside Map Grid:
• Start: 06–07 and 65–66
• Finish: 06–07 and 66–67

We've been told that many older residents tackle this
mb before dawn every morning, to practice Tai Chi at
top. For obvious reasons, we have not personally
ecked this out, but you are welcome to see for yourself!

To Get There

e trail starts under the Peak Tramway Station. At the intersection at the west end of
Peak Tramway Station, facing west, turn right on Peak Road, then sharp right down
stairs around and behind the Peak Tramway Station to a lane that heads down the
l and under the tramway tracks. This is the start of Old Peak Road.

Or, facing the Galleria, turn left onto Findlay Road. At the end of the Peak Tower,
e the left fork down Findlay Path, which leads to the intersection of Plantation Road
d Barker Road, at the Barker Road Tramway Station. Turn left and go under the tramway
cks to Old Peak Road.

If you took the stairs behind the Peak Tramway Station, you will pass the Old Peak
ad Rest Garden on your left. At this point you will have some nice views of the
rbor. Stay on Old Peak Road to the Tramway tracks. Turn left downhill.

Winding down the canyon, you pass benches where you can give your knees a
eak. Soon you will reach apartment complexes and an intersection, giving you some
HOICES:

Old Peak Road — straight
Tregunter Path — A sharp right along a level road takes you to May Road, which
leads to Magazine Gap Road (where you could pick up the Chatham Path and
Central Green Trail, Hike 1G). See Countryside Map Grid 06–07 and 66.

From this point on, the road is a two-way street, winding past residential apartme Press on to Hornsey Road, just below the May Road overpass.

To Continue to Hike

- Left on Hornsey Road to Conduit Road, then left on Conduit Road to Hatton R and the Morning Trail and Cheung Po Tsai Path, Hike 1B in reverse.
- As above, but right on Conduit Road to Chatham Path and Central Green Tr Hike 1G.

To Leave the Trail

- Turn right on Conduit Road for a short distance to the top of the escalator/stair the Mid-levels.

  Note: The escalator runs downhill only from 6:00 a.m. to 10:00 a.m.; at other tir you must take the stairs alongside.

- Follow Old Peak Road until it becomes Albany Road, intersecting with Robin. Road. Albany Road bisects the Hong Kong Zoological and Botanical Gardens route to Central.

G CHATHAM PATH AND CENTRAL GREEN TRAIL

𝐊 𝐍 𝐑 𝐒

...hatham Path winds down to Central through lush ...etation. One of two Green Trails in Hong Kong (the ...er is Wan Chai Green Trail, Hike 2A), the Central Green ...il includes educational signs along the way that point ... specific trees and plants, even common weeds. A short ...our off the trail takes you to a lovely little shrine. The ...er half of the hike passes through built up areas and ...s along the Peak Tramway tracks. At this point, the ...l is "green" more for its environmental information ...n for its shrubbery.

> Distance: 2.75 km/1.7 mi
> Difficulty: 2/5
> Time: 45 min
> Rise: 220 m
> N Map 1.2
> Countryside Map Grid:
> • Start: 06–07 and 65–66
> • Finish: 07–08 and 66–67

To Get There

...rt at the Peak Tramway Station. Facing the Galleria, turn left onto Findlay Road.

At the end of the Peak Tower, take the left fork down Findlay Path, which leads to ...ntation Road near Barker Road at the Barker Road Tramway Station. Here turn left ...Plantation Road then right on Barker Road. Follow Barker Road about 1 km/0.6 mi ...he old Victoria Hospital (1897) on the right. Tennis courts are set below street level ...he left. On the hospital lawn, marker No. 14 of the Central Green Trail points out a ...ping fig tree. See Countryside Map Grid 07–08 and 65–66.

Just beyond the tennis courts, Chatham Path descends on stairs on the left (north) ... of Barker Road. Signs in this section point out plants, explain hydrology theory ... discuss environmental issues.

Be sure to visit the charming shrine down a concrete path off to the left just before ...en Trail sign No. 10.

As you near May Road, the path splits. The right fork is a dead end, **so take the ...k to the left.** *Note: There are public toilets on the left and a telephone at May Road.*

Chatham Path ends at an early 1900s postbox. The Central Green Trail continues.

At May Road (and the May Road Tramway Station [95 m]) turn left and cross the ...dge over the tramway tracks; immediately turn right onto Clovelly Path, sharply ...vn the hill. Keep to Clovelly Path until you connect with Brewin Path, watching for ...re information signs.

Turn right on Brewin Path, a short distance to Cotton Tree Drive at Magazine Gap ...d. Cross the street at the traffic island and find stairs down, signed Tramway Path.

The path alternates between stairs and ramps, and runs directly alongside the P
Tramway tracks. Pass the MacDonnell Road Tramway Station, and a sign with histor
information about the tramway.

At MacDonnell Road, cross the road and turn right over the tramway tracks. St
down are clearly marked as the Tramway Path. This section is a bit steeper. After
pass St. Paul's Co-Educational College on your right, a last set of stairs takes you un
the tramway tracks to Kennedy Road.

Cross Kennedy Road and stay to the right of the tramway tracks. Follow
alternating stairs and ramps down this gentler slope. You will pass the World Wild
Fund for Nature, as well as the Kennedy Road Tramway Station. Keep going to
intersection of Garden Road and Lower Albert Road.

Along the lower trail, from Magazine Gap Road to the World Wildlife Fund build
Green Trail signs continue, discussing topics such as landscape planning and
trimming. Some of the signs are a bit obscured when landscaping work is overdue

To Continue to Hike

- Old Peak Road — Cross Garden Road and enter the Hong Kong Zoological
  Botanical Gardens, then walk through the Gardens to Albany Road. Turn lef
  Albany Road and walk up to the intersection with Old Peak Road at the tra
  circle near the Ladies' Recreation Club — Hike 1F in reverse.
- Morning Trail and Cheung Po Tsai Path — Cross Garden Road and enter the H
  Kong Zoological and Botanical Gardens, then walk through the Gardens to Alb
  Road. Take a left on Albany Road, then right at Robinson Road, and take the escal
  up to Conduit Road. Turn right and follow Conduit Road to the intersection v
  Kotewall and Hatton Roads, and go left (up) — Hike 1B in reverse.
  *Note: The escalator runs downhill from 6:00 a.m. to 10:00 a.m. and uphill at
  other times.*

To Leave the Trail

- You can leave the trail at any of the main roads you cross, such as May, Kenned
  MacDonnell Roads.
- Hong Kong Park — pass under Cotton Tree Drive across from the Garden R
  Tramway Station.
- Hong Kong Zoological and Botanical Gardens — cross Garden Road
- Central — cross Garden Road, turn right, cross Lower Albert Road, turn left c
  lane after passing St John's Cathedral. At the first opportunity turn right and fol
  Battery Path past the Court of Final Appeal gently down to Ice House Street a
  Queen's Road Central.
- Take the Peak Tramway back up. (Lazy bones!)

D K R S

H *PEAK LOOPS*

Map 1.2

The many short paths and lightly trafficked roads of the Peak can be combined for ~~diverse~~rse and charming hikes. This is good running territory too. Try some of these.

Mount Kellett Road *R S*

Special views on a 2 km/1.25 mi walk or run, especially if you detour to the Matilda Hospital (1907). Starting at the intersection at the west end of the Peak Tramway Station, facing west, turn left and walk along Peak Road. At the shopping center, stay on the upper pavement, where the road surface is marked Plunkett's Road. At the intersection, take the left fork (Plunkett's Road) then turn right over the overpass over Peak Road, and cross onto Mount Kellett Road. Follow Mount Kellett Road to the Matilda Hospital, taking a left turn down hill just after No. 14 Kellett (on the right). You should detour to the back of the hospital to enjoy the view. Return to Mount Kellett Road, walking up and down a hill to a gated paved path on the left, Homestead Road. This will return you to Peak Road near the overpass.

Plantation Road *R*

Another good loop, if hilly, for a walk or run with views and fancy houses. We estimate the following loop to be about 2 km/1.25 mi. At the Peak Tramway station, facing the Galleria, turn left onto Findlay Road. Stay on the right fork, Findlay Road, as it heads gently uphill, passing a sitting out area on the left — Tai Ping Shan, Lion's View Point Pavilion. There is usually an *al fresco* art gallery here — stick to the real views, a full sweep of the harbor. Findlay Road runs into Plantation Road. Turn right on Plantation a few feet before it intersects with Severn Road. At this point you can take a left on Severn Road (see below) or you can stay with Plantation upwards to Pollack's Path (which is a dead end). Plantation Road continues up hill then down to Plunkett's Road and Peak Road, turn right to return to the start.

Hospital and Lloyd Paths

Hospital Path, only a few hundred meters long, leads from Plantation Road to Barker Road (at the Victoria Hospital) crossing Severn Road en route. You can then follow Barker Road down for a scenic half mile or so and then take Lloyd Path from Barker Road back up. The loop should take no more than 45 minutes. Take

Findlay Road to Plantation Road (see Plantation Road, above). Go right (up
on Plantation Road then right again to stay on Plantation Road when it m
Severn Road. On the left side of the street, an unsigned path leads downhill —
is a short-cut to Hospital Path. A short distance further up the road, beyond
apartment driveway and just before No. 56, a concrete path runs left down un
the driveway. The sign for Hospital Path is somewhat buried in the thicke
bamboo.

Crossing Severn Road on the way (an Elizabeth II post box marks the crossi
the path emerges on Barker Road at the Victoria Hospital, no doubt the origi
the path's name. Chatham Path is across Barker Road (Hike 1G). Turn righ
walk along Barker Road for about 1 km/0.6 mi. Just to the east of No. 11 Barker
a tight curve, look for stairs on the right side of the road. There is a sign, Ll
Path, but it is a few feet up the path. The path is short, steep but with switchba
and has few views. It emerges at Severn Road near the Severn Road Service Reser
and Pumping Station. You can then return to the Peak by going right on Sev
Road to Plantation Road and on to Findlay Road.

- **Severn Road** Ⓡ Ⓢ Ⓒ
Severn Road circles Mount Gough, starting at Plantation Road and Findlay R
and reconnecting with Plantation Road at Pollack's Path. The views are drama
especially of the south side. Coming from Findlay, there is a slope down, a b
flat section, then a long slow climb, and a very steep little bit at the end. A g
choice for a run, Severn Road itself is about 1.5 km long (just under a mile)
find Severn Road, follow the directions for Plantation Road.

- **Bluff Path and Gough Hill Road**
These two routes make a short intense loop (perhaps 1 km/0.6 mi) starting
Peak Road downhill from Mount Kellett Road and ending near the fire statior
Peak Road. There are interesting houses and nice views on Gough Hill. Startin
the intersection at the west end of the Peak Tramway Station, facing west, turn
and walk up Peak Road. At the shopping center, stay on the lower pavem
where the road surface is marked Peak Road. Follow Peak Road under the over
to Gough Hill Road on the right. Take Gough Road on a loop, past the fire stat
then back up to rejoin Peak Road. Cross Peak Road and pick up Bluff Path on
other side, a bit further down. At the top of Bluff Path, take a right to Gough
Road. At the bottom of Gough Hill Road, detour to the lane on the left up past
police station for a quick look at a superb and not well-known view. A sign for
police station points the way.

If you prefer, stay on the road (which is now Plantation Road) to the next intersection. Here a left turn takes you back to Peak Road or if you prefer you can go right on Plantation Road.

You can also access Gough Hill Road just off Pollack's Path. For this hike, take Old Peak Road to Plunkett's Road (as in Mount Kellett Road above), right on Plantation Road then straight onto Plunkett's Path. The Peel Rise hike (Hike 1L) starts at Gough Hill Road by the Fire Station.

Craigmin Road

A nice path of about 0.5 km but it ends up quite far down on Peak Road so it is best to return the way you came. Starting at the intersection at the west end of the Peak Tramway Station, facing west, turn left and walk up Peak Road. At the shopping center, stay on the lower pavement, where the road surface is marked Peak Road. Follow Peak Road under the overpass to Gough Hill Road on the left. Start up Gough Road but quickly turn right downhill along Craigmin Road. (You could first take the lane parallel to Gough Road that leads up past the police station for a quick look at a superb and not well-known view. A sign for the police station points the way.)

1J POK FU LAM RESERVOIR FAMILY WALK

Our version of the trail combines Pok Fu Lam Reservoir Road, which winds downhill under a cooling canopy of trees, and Hong Kong Trail Section 1, also leafy and cool but not very scenic. Other Family Walks are much less challenging, as the climb up Pok Fu Lam Reservoir Road is steep. We would think twice about getting young kids out on this one, but it's a nice change of pace for adults. If you start at Pokfulam, it is a much easier hike.

Distance: 3.5 km/2.2 mi
Difficulty: 3/5
Time: 1 hr 30 min
Rise: 400 m
Map 1.3
Countryside Map Grid:
• Start and Finish:
  06–07 and 65–66
• Pok Fu Lam Reservoir R[
  ends at 04–05 and 65

To Get There

To access the trail, begin near the Peak Tramway Station. At the intersection at the w
end of the Tramway Station, facing west, turn left on Peak Road. After just a few ya
take Pok Fu Lam Reservoir Road downhill, behind a gate pole with a sign for Pok
Lam Country Park and marker T8110. The road is bordered by a stone retaining v
that is itself retained by the roots of a huge *ficus microcarpa* tree.

In about half an hour you will reach the JUNCTION for the Family Walk (a
marker T8112):

• **Pok Fu Lam Family Walk (Hong Kong Trail Section 1) — 3.5 km/2.2 mi; 1
  30 min — right**
• Pok Fu Lam Reservoir Road to Peel Rise (Hong Kong Trail Section 2) — 4.7 k
  2.9 mi; 1 hr 40 min — down the hill — see Hike 1K
• Peak Tramway Station via Lugard Road (Hong Kong Trail Section 1) — 6.8 k
  4.2 mi; 1 hr 50 min — right (also the Family Walk — Hike 1A)
• Pok Fu Lam Road — 1.1 km/0.7 mi; 15 min — ahead
• The Peak — 1.3 km/0.8 mi; 30 min — back

The trail contours along the hillside, weaving in and out of the canyons, alternat
between dirt and rock paving, following gentle rises and falls as it crosses many strea
and stream beds. It is mostly flat with steps scattered throughout. Trudge along ab
2.5 km/1.6 mi to a JUNCTION:

Pok Fu Lam Reservoir — 0.2 km/0.1 mi; 15 min — down steps to the left
Peak Tram via Lugard Road (Hong Kong Trail Section 1) — 4.5 km/2.8 mi;
1 hr 15 min — ahead
Chi Fu (a large housing estate, with amenities) — 3.5 km/2.2 mi; 1 hr 15 min —
back
The Peak via Pok Fu Lam Reservoir Road (Hong Kong Trail Section 1) — 3.75 km/
2.4 mi; 1 hr 15 min — back

Turn left and down a short flight of stairs then across a concrete berm to a grassy
a, cross the near corner to the left, and take about 100 stairs to Pok Fu Lam Reservoir
ad, and a signpost.

The Peak — 2.25 km/1.4 mi; 45 min — uphill
Peel Rise (Hong Kong Trail Section 2) — 5 km/3.2 mi; 1 hr 30 min
Chi Fu [Housing Estate] — 2.5 km/1.6 mi; 45 min
BBQ site and Family Walk
a can avoid the hill and leave the trail here, see To Leave the Trail.

When you are facing the signpost, all signs point to the right, uphill. A map board
e shows an Orienteering Course.

Follow the flat paved road along the west side of Pok Fu Lam Reservoir. On the
ekends you will see many people out strolling along, walking their dogs, feeding the
dfish or fishing. We once saw a kite (a native hawk) scavenging the lake for his
ner! Shortly you reach a bridge; cross and begin the climb up to the Peak. You come
oss a few small World War II buildings, now bricked up. After a wooden marker
h an evergreen tree and the letter O, stairs form a short cut to Hong Kong Trail
tion 2, en route to Peel Rise, Hike 1K. We don't know what the marker signifies.

Press on up the road a short distance to the next set of signs and several CHOICES:
the left:

The Peak — 1.5 km/0.9 mi; 30 min — ahead
Pok Fu Lam Road — 1 km/0.6 mi; 15 min — back

the right:
Peel Rise (Hong Kong Trail Section 2) — 4.5 km/2.8 mi; 1 hr 30 min — right
Chi Fu — right

Less than 0.5 km/0.3 mi later you are back at the junction that started the Family
lk.

To Continue to Hike

- Hong Kong Trail Section 2, Hike 1K — back 0.5 km/0.3 mi to the junction.

To Leave the Trail

- Walk up Pok Fu Lam Reservoir Road to the Peak.
- To leave the trail at its Pok Fu Lam end, at the intersection with Pok Fu L
  Reservoir Road, turn downhill and pass through the gate and down the road, p
  a University of Hong Kong building on the right. Next, the Lady Maclehe
  P.H.A.B. on your left (with a drinks machine), then the Pok Fu Lam Jockey C
  Public Riding School. (How many two-story riding stables have you seen?) Bu
  and taxis are plentiful on Pok Fu Lam Road; see the Hub description for m
  details.

To Access the Trail from Pok Fu Lam

If you wish to do the hike from Pok Fu Lam, take a bus or taxi to Pok Fu Lam Reserv
Road off Pok Fu Lam Road, near Queen Mary Hospital. Parking is available at Chi
and at Queen Mary Hospital, and people do park on Pok Fu Lam Reservoir Road, illega
See Hub Amenities for bus listings.

Enter the park through the gate pole and take the steps up left immediately a
the pole. At the top of the first flight of steps a blue sign reads "Pok Fu Lam Serv
Reservoir No. 1."

HONG KONG TRAIL SECTION 2 — POK FU LAM RESERVOIR ROAD TO PEEL RISE

K

he lovely trail, much of it wooded, wends its way ough the hills above Pok Fu Lam. There are only a few ws along the way but towards the finish the trail has ne stupendous views of the south side of the Island: erdeen, Ap Lei Chau, the typhoon shelter, the channel l the outlying islands. At the end, heading down into erdeen, there are many steps, some up but many more vn.

Distance: 4.5 km/2.8 mi
Difficulty: 3/5
Time: 1 hr 30 min
Rise: 100 m
Map 1.3
Countryside Map Grid:
• Start: 06–07 and 65–66
• Finish: 06–07 and 64

To Get There

e beginning of the hike is the same as Hike 1J, Pok Fu Lam Reservoir Family Walk.

To access the trail, begin at the intersection at the west end of the Tramway Station, ing west, and turn left on Peak Road. After just a few yards, take the road downhill, iind a gate pole with a sign for Pok Fu Lam Country Park and marker T8110. The d is bordered by a stone retaining wall that is itself retained by the roots of a huge s microcarpa tree.

In about half an hour you will reach the first of several JUNCTIONS (marker 112):

Pok Fu Lam Reservoir Road to Peel Rise (Hong Kong Trail Section 2) — 4.7 km/2.9 mi; 1 hr 40 min — ahead

Pok Fu Lam Family Walk — 3.5 km/2.2 mi; 1 hr 30 min — right — Hike 1J

Pok Fu Lam Road — 1.1 km/0.7 mi; 15 min — ahead

Peak Tramway Station via Lugard Road (Hong Kong Trail Section 1) — 6.8 km/ 4.2 mi; 1 hr 50 min — right (also the Family Walk — Hike 1A)

The Peak — 1.3 km/0.8 mi; 30 min — back

Very shortly you will arrive at a second major JUNCTION:

the right:

Hong Kong Trail Section 2 — Pok Fu Lam Reservoir Road to Peel Rise — 4.5 km/2.8 mi; 1 hr 30 min — left

Pok Fu Lam Road — 1 km/0.6 mi; 15 min — ahead

The Peak — 1.5 km/0.9 mi; 30 min — back

A marker indicates that the Hong Kong Trail (Section 1) and Pok Fu Lam Reservoir Family Walk are back up the hill — Hikes 1A, 1J.

On the left:

- **Peel Rise (Hong Kong Trail Section 2) — 4.5 km/2.8 mi; 1 hr 30 min — left**
- Chi Fu (a large housing estate, with amenities) — left

Take the paved road to the left. The first Hong Kong Trail marker is H015, a which you pass the Hong Kong Water Works Pok Fu Lam Service Reservoir No (1977) on your left side. Nearby, stairs down to the right lead to Pok Fu Lam Reserv Road. A short distance up the road on your right there is a picnic site that is wort detour for a splendid view (rare on this hike) even if you aren't picnicking. On the a signpost for a JUNCTION:

- **Peel Rise (Hong Kong Trail Section 2) — 4 km/2.5 mi; no time given but i 1 hr 15 min — left**
- Chi Fu [Housing Estate] — 1.25 km/0.8 mi — left
- The Peak (Hong Kong Trail Section 1) — 7.25 km/4.5 mi; no time given but i 2 hr 15 min — back
- Pok Fu Lam Road — 1.5 km /0.9 mi; 30 min — back
- The road you are on, a reservoir access lane, continues about 0.5 km/0.3 m another water works facility.

Clamber up the stone stairs (100 or so) and turn left at the paved road at the t If you wish, detour to visit a view compass with outstanding vistas looking out over shipping channel, by crossing the paved road and turning right down the stairs.

Go on up the road, past a little fitness area and more BBQ spots, to marker H0 where the road begins to slope down. You soon reach a small stone paved area on right, popular for Tai Chi, and a sign for a picnic site on the left. The JUNCTI marker reads:

- **Peel Rise (Hong Kong Trail Section 2) — 3.75 km/2.4 mi; 1 hr 15 min — ahe**
- Chi Fu [Housing Estate] — 1 km/0.6 mi; 15 min — ahead
- Pok Fu Lam Reservoir Road — 0.75 km/0.5 mi; 15 min — back
- Unmarked, another possibility is to take a sharp left onto a paved lane. Here y can either:
  - take the lane for a big climb to a view, worth the effort, at a dead end ab 350 meters up the side of Mount Kellett (501 m) — about 1 km/0.6 mi; min
  - take the lane about 200 meters, down and then back up a hill, then take a trail to the right. This wooded undulating dirt path is used by horseback rid from the Pok Fu Lam Jockey Club stables. It has better views than the Ho Kong Trail and saves you part of a hill. It rejoins Hong Kong Trail Section 2 marker H018.

At the bottom of the hill, past a lovely grove of trees, you will find a map board and ̣ilet, a bridge over a stream and another JUNCTION:

Hong Kong Trail Section 2 — Pok Fu Lam Reservoir Road to Peel Rise — 3.3 km/2 mi; 1 hr — left

Chi Fu [Housing Estate] — 0.6 km/0.4 mi; 15 min — ahead

Pok Fu Lam Reservoir Road — 1.2 km/0.75 mi; 30 min — back

Turn left along the level path. As the road curves to the left around a small pavilion, ̣ trails lead to the right within a few yards of each other. A worthwhile detour, the trails ̣n a circular side path to an old gun emplacement, a covered picnic area, and a view.

Continuing on, a new, rock-paved trail winds gently upward, then veers left on a ̣crete path uphill to marker H018. Just before this marker, the horse trail joins from ̣ left (see marker H016); steps down to the right lead to a catchwater.

CHOICES:

Stay on the trail — a paved road.

Loop back along the horse trail to return to Pok Fu Lam Reservoir Road.

The road now turns downhill in a tree-shaded area. You pass a very nice waterfall. ̣p an eye out for some quick views of Lamma, Cheung Chau and other outlying ̣nds. The trail will generally trend down, leveling off in sections. A brief climb leads ̣ to a flat wooded section that is cool and shady, giving you the feeling that you are ̣ remote area, and yet your ears begin to tell you the city is close at hand.

Near marker H021, the path breaks open for views of Lamma Island. The road ̣pes down to an open area, and stops abruptly. **An emergency phone is on the right**. ̣e road becomes steps down. Look left through the walls of the catchwater for ̣athtaking views of Aberdeen, Ap Lei Chau and the harbor; the drop is precipitous ̣d may be literally breathtaking for those prone to vertigo.

̣te: *There is a government sign warning that the next section of the trail (until you reach the level area of the catchwater) is dangerous and suitable only for the experienced and well-equipped hiker. It's not really that bad, but it is steep with many irregular steps and some quite exposed sections.*

Start down the (many) stairs and the path becomes fairly open. Dainty ferns and ̣utiful pink flowers decorate the path. Aberdeen Harbor is in full view; look for the ̣ing boats and the little junks. You can't miss the colorful Jumbo Floating Restaurant ̣the middle.

At marker H022, there is a JUNCTION:

Hong Kong Trail Section 2 — Pok Fu Lam Reservoir Road to Peel Rise — 1.5 km/0.9 mi; 15 min — left

Wah Fu [Housing Estate] — 0.6 km/0.4 mi; 15 min — straight

Pok Fu Lam Reservoir Road — 3 km/1.9 mi; 1 hr — back

Be prepared for many steep steps. The city hustle and bustle, mostly traffic no
reasserts itself. There are power lines above and an enormous cemetery on the hil
front of you. An abrupt right takes you down more steps, several switchbacks,
across a waterfall. The views are still amazing. At marker H023, two more switchba
will bring you to a signpost. Be sure to stay on the trail by turning right and down e
more steps. Then turn left and walk along the catchwater.

On our last hike, this section was a bit overgrown, and you may wonder if y
really are in the right spot, but you are. Just keep going and enjoy the lovely waterfa

After marker H024, a JUNCTION:

- **Hong Kong Trail (unmarked) — ahead**
- Aberdeen — a metal sign informs that stairs down lead to Aberdeen, a 15-min
  walk. Several hundred stairs deposit you at the back of the Hung Fuk Court,
  Tin Wan Street, west of Aberdeen.

Stairs up to the left appear to lead to Matilda Hospital on Mount Kellett, see H
1H. We left this mystery for you to explore.

Press on to marker H025, crossing up and over a stream on a huge concrete dam
arrive at a wide paved road — Peel Rise Road (not signed). On the right, a signp
announces your CHOICES:

- Wan Chai Gap (Hong Kong Trail Section 3) — 6.5 km/4 mi; 1 hr 45 min—
  across the catchwater
  Note: the stairs up to the right are a steep short cut to Hong Kong Trail Section 3.
- Peak Road — 2.25 km/1.4 mi; 45 min — left across the catchwater
- Aberdeen — 1.25 km/0.8 mi; 15 min — ahead on Peel Rise Road
- Aberdeen Country Park — about 1.5 km/0.9 mi; 15 min — ahead on Peel F
  Road a short way, then bear left on the catchwater — Hike 2E
- Pok Fu Lam Reservoir Road (Hong Kong Trail Section 2) — 4.5 km/2.8 mi; 1
  30 min — back

To Leave the Trail

- Aberdeen — 1.25 km/0.8 mi; 15 min — ahead, down Peel Rise Road

To Access the Trail from Aberdeen

Aberdeen is a major bus and minibus interchange. From Central take bus No. 70; fr
Stanley take bus No. 73 or 973.

Parking is available off Aberdeen Reservoir Road.

From the bus terminus, walk up Aberdeen Main Road (away from the harbor
Peel Rise Road on the left, then continue on Peel Rise Road for about 1.25 km/0.8
15 min. If you prefer, you can take bus No. 7 or 76 or minibus No. 4C up the hill.

HONG KONG TRAIL SECTION 3 — PEEL RISE TO WAN CHAI GAP

L

ℝ

fter an initial steep downhill stretch along Peel Rise to ch the trailhead, the trail itself is largely level and tree ed with lots of streambeds. This is a good walk for a : day, when you want to get out but don't want a lot of ... There are some nice views but this is not one of the ·st scenic trails. The trail winds in and out of two yons around Tin Wan Shan (252 m). Joggers will find s an excellent jogging trail. However, be prepared: at end of your hike to return to the Peak you must drag urself back uphill to Wan Chai Gap along the equally ep (but shorter) Aberdeen Reservoir Road.

> Distance: 6.5 km/4 mi
> Difficulty: 2/5
> Time: 1 hr 45 min
> Rise: 150 m
> Map 1.3
> Countryside Map Grid:
> • Start: 06–07 and 64
> • Finish: 08 and 64

To Get There

rting at the intersection at the west end of the Peak Tramway Station, facing west, n left and walk up Peak Road. At the shopping center, stay on the upper pavement, ere the road surface is marked Plunkett's Road. At the intersection, take the left fork unkett's Road), turn right to the overpass over Peak Road, and then turn immediately t downhill (do not take Mount Kellett Road). You are now on Peel Rise.

Continue down the hill, past Gough Hill Path and the Fire Station on the left. Note ; gnarled tree roots, holding up the concrete walls. The lovely Peel Rise Rest Garden nestled on your right. At Wing On Villas, the road ends and the trail begins.

Follow the trail as it switches backs and forth down the hill under a canopy of es. After about 15 minutes you will reach a signpost, a picnic area on the right, and a NCTION:

Hong Kong Trail Section 3 — Wan Chai Gap — 5.9 km/3.7 mi; 1 hr 45 min — left.

Aberdeen via Peel Rise — 1.8 km/1.1 mi; 30 min — straight — Hike 1M

Peak Road — 1.8 km/1.1 mi; 45 min — back

Stroll or jog along through pleasant woods punctuated by steam beds, to marker ▶30, some power lines, and another JUNCTION:

- **Aberdeen Reservoir Road — 3.25 km/2 mi; 1 hr — straight ahead**
- Peel Rise — 0.25 km/0.1 mi; 15 min — stairs right for a short cut to Peel Rise at junction with Hong Kong Trail Section 2 from which you can take the Hong K[o] Trail or return to the Peak (about 30 min).
- The Peak (Peel Rise) — 1.5 km/0.9 mi; 30 min — back (probably would t[a] 45 min)

The next 2 km curve in and out of canyons. Look hard for some peek-a-boo vie[w] of Aberdeen Harbor (over a water treatment plant) including the Jumbo Float[ing] Restaurant and the Aberdeen Marina Club. Before marker H033, you will have view[ed] Mount Cameron (439 m) to the left, Aberdeen Reservoir and Mount Nicholson (430[m]) in the far distance, and Brick Hill (284 m) to the far right.

After marker H034, cross a few streams with large rocks and waterfalls, then p[ass] **an emergency phone** and then cross another stream bed, reaching a vertical catchwa[ter] and a JUNCTION:

- **Aberdeen Upper Reservoir — 1 km/0.6 mi; 30 min — straight ahead**
- Watford Road — 0.25 km/0.2 mi; 15 min — up and to the left. Watford Road lea[ds] to Guilford Road, which joins Peak Road just above the intersection of Stub[bs] Coombe and Magazine Gap Roads. There is a small shopping center with a Wellco[me] Store. See Countryside Map Grid 07–08 and 64–65.
- Peel Rise — 4 km/2.4 mi; 1 hr — back

Just beyond marker H035, take in the view of Mount Kellett (501 m) on the l[eft]. Further on, the view expands to include Mount Gough on the right, stretching to [the] Aberdeen Typhoon Shelter and the shipping channel, Ap Lei Chau, and Lamma Isla[nd] in the distance.

Another JUNCTION (H036):

- **Wan Chai Gap — 1.5 km/0.9 mi; 30 min — ahead**
- Aberdeen Reservoir — (no distance noted, but it is 0.3 km/0.2 mi; 15 min) — [a] short cut to the Upper Reservoir at Aberdeen Reservoir Road — right
- Peel Rise — 4.5 km/2.8 mi; 1 hr 15 min — back

Enjoy views of Deepwater Bay, and the fancy houses on Deepwater Bay Ro[ad]. Soon the trail begins to parallel Aberdeen Reservoir Road. Reaching marker H037, has[ten] down several steps to find a map board, a signpost, and Aberdeen Reservoir Road.

🚶 To Continue to Hike

- Upper Aberdeen Reservoir — 1.16 km/0.75 mi; 20 min — down Aberdeen Reserv[oir] Road to the right

- Black's Link via Lady Clementi's Ride and Middle Gap Road (Hong Kong Trail Section 4) — 5.56 km/3.5 mi; 1 hr 40 min — across Aberdeen Reservoir Road and to the right; see Hikes 2C, 3H
- Peel Rise — 5.5 km/3.5 mi; 1 hr 30 min — back (note discrepancy from marker at start)
- Detour to the Morning Walkers' Garden on the left side of the road.

To Leave the Trail

- Wan Chai Gap — 0.6 km/0.4 mi; 15 min — march back uphill on Aberdeen Reservoir Road or Peel Rise. See Hikes 1M, 2E. If you want to walk all the way back to the Peak from Wan Chai Gap, we recommend taking Coombe Road to Peak Road, then Barker Road, a short way up Peak Road; see Hike 1H.
- Aberdeen — down Aberdeen Reservoir Road to Aberdeen

To Access the Trail from Aberdeen

Aberdeen is a major bus and minibus interchange. From Central take bus No. 70; from Stanley take bus No. 73 or 973.

Parking is available off Aberdeen Reservoir Road.

From the bus terminus, walk up Aberdeen Main Road (away from the harbor) then bear right on Aberdeen Reservoir Road up a big hill to the entrance to the Aberdeen Country Park, where you can continue up Aberdeen Reservoir Road to Hong Kong Trail Section 3. If you prefer, you can take bus No. 7 or 76 or minibus No. 4C up the hill.

1M PEEL RISE — THE PEAK TO ABERDEEN ®️ ⑩

So you want to get to Aberdeen but not on the bus? A walk down Peel Rise, a paved lane that wanders downhill under a canopy of trees, then alongside a stream and finally though an historic cemetery, is a delightful, scenic way to visit the south side. Be prepared for a long descent or ascent, depending on the direction you take. A good choice for a run, if you don't mind hills.

> Distance: 3.6 km/2.2 mi
> Difficulty: 2/5
> Time: 1 hr
> Rise: 400 m
> Map 1.3
> Countryside Map Grid:
> • Start: 06–07 and 65–66
> • Finish: 06–07 and 63–64

🥾 To Get There

Up to the first junction, this hike is the same as Hike 1L.

Starting at the intersection at the west end of the Peak Tramway Station, facing west, turn left and walk up Peak Road. At the shopping center, stay on the upper pavement, where the road surface is marked Plunkett's Road. At the intersection, take the left fork (Plunkett's Road), turn right to the overpass over Peak Road, and then turn immediately left downhill (do not take Mount Kellett Road). You are now on Peel Rise.

Continue down the hill, past Gough Hill Path and the fire station on the left. Note the gnarled tree roots, holding up the concrete walls. The lovely Peel Rise Rest Garden is nestled on your right. At Wing On Villas, the road ends and the trail begins.

Follow the trail as it switches back and forth down the hill under a canopy of trees. After about 15 minutes you will reach a signpost, a picnic area on the right, and a JUNCTION:

- **Aberdeen via Peel Rise— 1.8 km/1.1 mi; 30 min — straight**
- Hong Kong Trail Section 3 — Wan Chai Gap — 5.9 km/3.7 mi; 1 hr 45 min— left — Hike 1L. This section is also part of Lady Clementi's Ride; see Hike 3H for the rest of the "Ride."
- Peak Road — 1.8 km/1.1 mi; 45 min — back

Walk down the road, crossing over the stream and following it down to another road, a map board, and another JUNCTION:

- **Aberdeen — 1.25 km/0.8 mi; 15 min — left on Peel Rise Road**
- Aberdeen Country Park — about 1.5 km/0.9 mi; 15 min — left on Peel Rise Road a short way then bear left on the catchwater — Hike 2E

Pok Fu Lam Reservoir Road (Hong Kong Trail Section 2) — 4.5 km/2.8 mi;
1 hr 30 min — right
Wan Chai Gap (Hong Kong Trail Section 3) — 6.5 km/4 mi; 1 hr 45 min — back
Note: the stairs up to the right are a steep short cut back to Hong Kong Trail Section 3.
Peak Road — 2.25 km/1.4 mi; 45 min — back

Peel Rise Road winds through shaded trees and past the entrance to Saint Peter's
ondary School, then through a very large cemetery, which is well worth exploring.

To Leave the Trail

en you are through exploring, return to Peel Rise Road. Proceed down hill and turn
t onto Aberdeen Reservoir Road; you soon join Aberdeen Main Road in the heart of
rdeen. Go all the way down Aberdeen Main Road and bear right at the bottom to get
he main bus terminus.

Access the Trail from Aberdeen

rdeen is a major bus and minibus interchange. From Central take bus No. 70; from
nley take bus No. 73 or 973.
    Parking is available off Aberdeen Reservoir Road.
    From the bus terminus, walk up Aberdeen Main Road (away from the harbor)
n take Peel Rise Road to the left. Immediately upon entering the road, take the right
k uphill.

1N MOUNT DAVIS TRAIL Ⓚ Ⓡ Ⓢ

This is a little known but worthwhile hike, with a good hill for a workout and beautiful views. Historical as well, Mount Davis (Mo Sing Leng) (269 m) is dotted with ruins of World War II defenses. One of the best kept secrets in town, the Youth Hostel at the top is a scenic rest stop where you can buy a snack. There also is a short detour that is suitable for running.

Distance: 3.75 km/2.4 mi
Difficulty: 2/5 road; 4/5 st
Time: 1 hr
Rise: 250 m
 Map 1.4
Countryside Map Grid:
• Start and Finish:
  03–04 and 66–67

You can approach Mount Davis a few different ways. We think the best routing is along the Reservoir Access Road (which intersects with Mount Davis Road) to Mount Davis Path, about a two-hour roundtrip, which we describe in detail below, along with some alternatives.

🚩 To Get There

Mount Davis Road intersects with Pok Fu Lam Road near the two huge cemeterie Pok Fu Lam.

By Bus:

Bus No. 40 or 40M from Admiralty or No. 94 from Aberdeen on Pok Fu Lam Roa Mount Davis Road or to the Chinese Christian Cemetery. From the cemetery, wa short distance downhill on Pok Fu Lam Road to the Chinese Gate on the left, go through the gate down the path, then take a left at Mount Davis Road.

Bus No. 3A from Central Ferry Piers (to Felix Villas) or minibus No. 54 fr Exchange Square or the ferry piers. These run down Mount Davis Road. Get off at On Li stop by the Chiu Yuen Cemetery.

By Car:

Take a cab, parking is not available.

On Foot:

Pik Shan Path to the Chinese Gate, then follow directions in "By Bus," above. See Hike

Walking down Mount Davis Road you have two CHOICES:
• **Begin the trail by climbing up the Mount Davis Service Fresh Water Reserv Access Road, which is on the right about five minutes from the start, and marked by a sign and crossed by a metal gate pole.**
• Mount Davis Road to Mount Davis Path, avoiding the reservoir.

Climb up to the reservoir, turn left, and follow the path along the reservoir wall. At far corner of the wall follow the steep road down, which leads to Mount Davis Path.

CHOICES:

Mount Davis Path — right

Victoria Road — left

Ascending Mount Davis Path, which is well-marked, follow the signs for the youth tel. You will arrive at an abandoned toilet block and picnic area.

CHOICES:

Mount Davis Path — ahead

Steps behind the toilet block go up to the top or down to Victoria Road.

Still on the path (about 30 min from the start), you arrive at a fork in the road and ne CHOICES:

Stay on Mount Davis Path as it curves left

The right hand fork leads down about a half mile, to a dead end. This would be a good stretch to run if you are looking for a fuller workout.

You may encounter some wild dogs; on the two occasions we went they were all k and no bite but be careful (see "What you should know"). You can buy drinks and cks at the hostel. On the back lawn of the youth hostel, rest for a moment to enjoy busy harbor views. You can climb further to the very top of Mount Davis (269 m), ere there are a number of abandoned buildings and some radio towers. Judging by numerous plastic BBs in the grass, the area is popular with war gamers on weekends. e map shows a path down to the cemetery but it is lost in the underbrush.

Back on the road, shortly after the end of the hostel fence, take stairs down to the ht, a short cut to Mount Davis Path, intersecting just above the toilet block.

CHOICES:

Continue on the steps to Victoria Road through the old Mount Davis Cottage area.

Return to Mount Davis Road. A left turn on Mount Davis Road takes you back to the start.

Alternatives

To access the trail from Victoria Road, start at the intersection on the western tip of the Island where Victoria Road and Mount Davis Road meet. You can take the No. 5A bus from Happy Valley via Queen's Road to the roundabout. Walk past the roundabout (towards Central) and you will shortly see Mount Davis Path up to the right.

2. For another approach you can take bus No. 5A or M47 and get off just before
    Island West transfer station (across from Serene Court). Go up the path thro
    the Mount Davis Cottage Area village climbing up next to a wide conc
    catchwater. The path is wooded with concrete steps and will intersect with Mc
    Davis Path about half way up.

P *PIK SHAN PATH*

Ⓡ

k Shan Path is included for three reasons, none of them
ch related to scenic hiking. First, it's a good running
l. Second, it's a good way to get to Mount Davis (Hike
) on foot. Third, it's a mystery, as no map we have seen
tifies Pik Shan (in English anyway). A shady flat path,
n pretty forest in only a few parts, this hike is utilitarian,
charming. Be warned that there is a bit of a climb to
up to the start. We describe the path from Kotewall
d, but it can also be accessed from Pok Fu Lam Road
from University Drive, see Alternatives.

> Distance: 3 km/1.9 mi
> Difficulty: 1/5
> Time: 30 min
> Rise: negligible
> **Ⓝ** Map 1.4
> Countryside Map Grid:
> • Start: 05–06 and 66–67
> • Finish: 04–05 and 65–66

To Get There

Bus:

No. 13 from the Star Ferry stops at the intersection of Kotewall, Hatton and Conduit
ds.

Foot:

rning Trail (Hike 1B) or Hong Kong Trail Section 1 (Hike 1A)

Car:

king is available at Hong Kong University Campus.

The path starts on Kotewall Road. Walk uphill (away from Central) and take steps
vn after the toilet block and across the Road from No. 17 Kotewall. The mystery
ins here, at the sign:

"To Pik Shan Pavilion" — you never arrive there!

Taking the steps down, turn left along the flat shady dirt path, crossing a few
:ams as you go. The Central and Western District Council has made a significant
estment in benches along the trail. After about 0.5 km/0.3 mi, you will see a brick
l and steps down to the right.

JUNCTION:

Stay on the path.

The 100 or so stairs to the right pass a little garden and shrine, then dead-end at a
path. The right turn is a steep lane to Water Supplies Department Elliot Number

Two Salt Water Reservoir and tennis courts belonging to Hong Kong Univer
The lane emerges at the Elliot Pumping Station 1987, on University Drive r
next to the University Student Union Building. The left turn leads to a stone
to even, nicely spaced steps up. After 35 steps up, about 300 stairs down, pa
pavilion, deposit you at the petrol station on Pok Fu Lam Road at Pokfield R
See Countryside Map Grid 04–05 and 66–67.

At this point, blue painted marks measure off the meters and the trail bed beco
concrete tiles. There are no views, but lots of benches and pavilions and signboards
the Morning Walkers' Club. At one point you may find a huge abacus hanging
small shelter, perhaps for counting up the miles clocked by the Club members. A
the 600-meter mark, there is a sign on the left, pointing up and down steps:

- **Unmarked — ahead**
- Hatton Road/Pinewood Battery — up
- Pokfield Road — down

See Hike 1B, the Morning Trail and Cheung Po Tsai Path for details on these optio

Stay on the path. Near the trail mid point, at marker 750, a JUNCTION:

- **Your route — ahead — is unmarked.**
- Lung Fu Shan Planting Site Number 1— left
- Hatton Road/Pinewood Battery — left
- The Peak — 3 km/1.9 mi; 1 hr — left

See Hike 1B, the Morning Trail and Cheung Po Tsai Path for details on these optio

The trail can be left (or accessed) near marker 850 on steps down to Pok Fu
Road at No. 94, Y.Y. Mansions.

Continuing along the trail, towards Pok Fu Lam, you come to a bridge ov
canyon. Before the bridge, a path leads up the side of the streambed to a quiet s
After passing the Chinese Gate to the Chinese Christian Cemetery, situated below
on Pok Fu Lam Road, meander in and out of the woods to a large building with a 1(
meter marker painted on the wall and stairs down to the right. You are at Pok Fu L
Road just east of the turn for Queen Mary Hospital, Sassoon Road and Bisney Road
the Bisney Road bus stop.

🏃 *To Continue to Hike*

- Mount Davis — cross Pok Fu Lam Road and enter the Chinese Gate to Mo
  Davis Road; see Hike 1N.
- Doubling back, you can follow the signs for the Peak to the many trails u
  Victoria Gap; see Hike 1B, Morning Trail and Cheung Po Tsai Path.

To Leave the Trail

es and taxis are plentiful on Pok Fu Lam Road.

Alternatives

You can get to the trail from Hong Kong Trail Section 1, turning right after marker H007.

To access from Pok Fu Lam Road at the Bisney Road bus stop, take the stairs from the bus stop up to a small building. Walk behind the building and up more stairs to a concrete path alongside a wall to the left.

To access at Pok Fu Lam Road No. 94, take a left at the fire hydrant and climb about 200 steps up.

To access at Pokfield and Pok Fu Lam Roads, take the stairs next to the gas station.

WAN CHAI GAP

he assortment of hikes radiating from Wan Chai Gap, in the middle of Hong Kong
nd, ranges from flat Bowen Road to steep Wan Chai Gap Road. Wan Chai Gap gives
access to all of Aberdeen Country Park with its beautiful reservoirs and diverse
ls. You can mix and match trails and then work your way back to the gap. Many of
hikes are also reasonable hikes for children and runners.

Map 2.1 and 2.2

untryside Map Grid: 08–09 and 65–66

To Get There

Bus:

s No. 15 from Central or the Star Ferry, about a 30 min trip

Foot:

From Wan Chai via Wan Chai Gap Road; see Hike 2A

From Aberdeen via Aberdeen Reservoir Road (Hike 2E) or Peel Rise (Hike 1M)

Via Bowen Road to Wan Chai Gap Road; see Hike 2B

Car:

t easy — there is some street parking on Mount Cameron Road at Wan Chai Gap,
d some more behind the playground on Coombe Road, across from Wan Chai Gap
k, but it is limited and tends to fill up quickly. See Hike 2B for parking near Bowen
ad. There is plentiful parking in Aberdeen.

2A WAN CHAI GAP ROAD AND WAN CHAI GAP GREEN TRAIL **N P**

Jungle to the city in half an hour! This very steep, lush trail drops right down to Queen's Road East bisecting Bowen Road (Hike 2B) on the way. A Green Trail, the way is marked with plaques identifying plants and points of interest. For a good aerobic challenge, do this one in reverse.

Distance: 1.4 km/0.9 mi	Difficulty: 3/5	Time: 30 min
Rise: 100 m	Map 2.1	
Countryside Map Grid: • Start and Finish: 08–09 and 65–66		

2B BOWEN ROAD **F D K S R X**

Bowen is one of the few flat (almost) roads in Hong Kong, so it is a favorite choice for jogging, kids, older folks and strollers. There is a fitness course along the eastern portion. The views are grand. For an extra bonus there are many small shrines along the way.

Distance: 4 km/2.5 mi	Difficulty: 1/5	Time: 45 min
Rise: negligible	Map 2.1	
Countryside Map Grid: • Start: 09–10 and 65 • Finish: 07–08 and 65–66		

2C BLACK'S LINK **D K R X**

A steady but gentle climb through Middle Gap, Black's Link provides good views to the north and to the south side of the Island. It is a wide paved path, popular for running. As it gently winds down to Deep Water Bay Road, around the corner from Wong Nai Chung Gap, there are lovely views of Aberdeen and beyond. Aptly named Black's Link is a handy connection to other hikes.

Distance: 3.2 km/2 mi	Difficulty: 2/5	Time: 1 hr
Rise: 50 m	Map 2.1	
Countryside Map Grid: • Start: 08–09 and 65–66 • Finish: 10–11 and 64		

2D MIDDLE GAP ROAD **R**

Not really a hike in itself, Middle Gap Road is a good link/short cut to other hikes. The scenery on Middle Gap Road is scrillionaire mansions. From Middle Gap Road you can reach:

- Black's Link — Hike 2C
- Lady Clementi's Ride — Hike 3H
- Aberdeen Country Park Hikes — Hike 2E
- Hong Kong Trail Section 4 — Wan Chai Gap to Wan Nai Chung Gap — Hike

Distance: 2.3 km/1.4 mi	Difficulty: 2/5	Time: 30 min
Rise: negligible	Map 2.1	
Countryside Map Grid: • Start: 08–09 and 65–66 • Finish: 08–09 and 64–65		

ABERDEEN COUNTRY PARK HIKES 🅕🅓🅚🅝🅢🅡 🅨 🅜

Great for both children and adults, there is a lot to explore in Aberdeen Country
k. It's a super spot for picnics, too, but claim your spot early on weekends. No trail
e is terribly difficult and they all interconnect, so just have a fun time exploring. The
vernment has laid out four clearly marked trails, which we describe here; you can
x and match.

See specific hike write-ups for distances and times.

Map 2.2

Countryside Map Grid 07–09 and 63–65.

HONG KONG TRAIL SECTION 4 — WAN CHAI GAP TO WONG NAI CHUNG GAP 🅝 🅡 🅨

This section of the Hong Kong Trail has long, flat, very scenic stretches, which are
ed with steep climbs on each end. There are excellent views to the south of the Island.
he end, you can see the crush of cars heading into the Aberdeen Tunnel, which runs
th/south under Middle Gap. Part of the Trail overlaps Lady Clementi's Ride.

Distance: 7.5 km/4.7 mi	Difficulty: 2/5	Time: 2 hr
Rise: 200 m	Map 2.1	
Countryside Map Grid: • Start: 08–09 and 65–66 • Finish: 10–11 and 64		

▶ Hub Amenities

Wan Chai Gap there is a park, a snack bar, toilets, a playground and the Police
iseum. Or you can finish your hike by walking down Wan Chai Gap Road (Hike 2A)
Wan Chai, with plenty of snack shops and restaurants. Aberdeen also has many
tions for a stop, including the Jumbo Floating Restaurant.

Access from Aberdeen

erdeen is a major bus and minibus interchange. From Central take bus No. 70; from
nley take bus No. 73 or 973.

Parking is available off Aberdeen Reservoir Road.

From the bus terminus, walk up Aberdeen Main Road (away from the harbor)
n bear right on Aberdeen Reservoir Road up a big hill to the entrance to the Aberdeen
untry Park; see Hike 2E. If you prefer you can take bus No. 7 or 76 or minibus No.
up the hill.

Alternatives

dy Clementi's Ride (Hike 3H) can also be accessed from Hub 2.

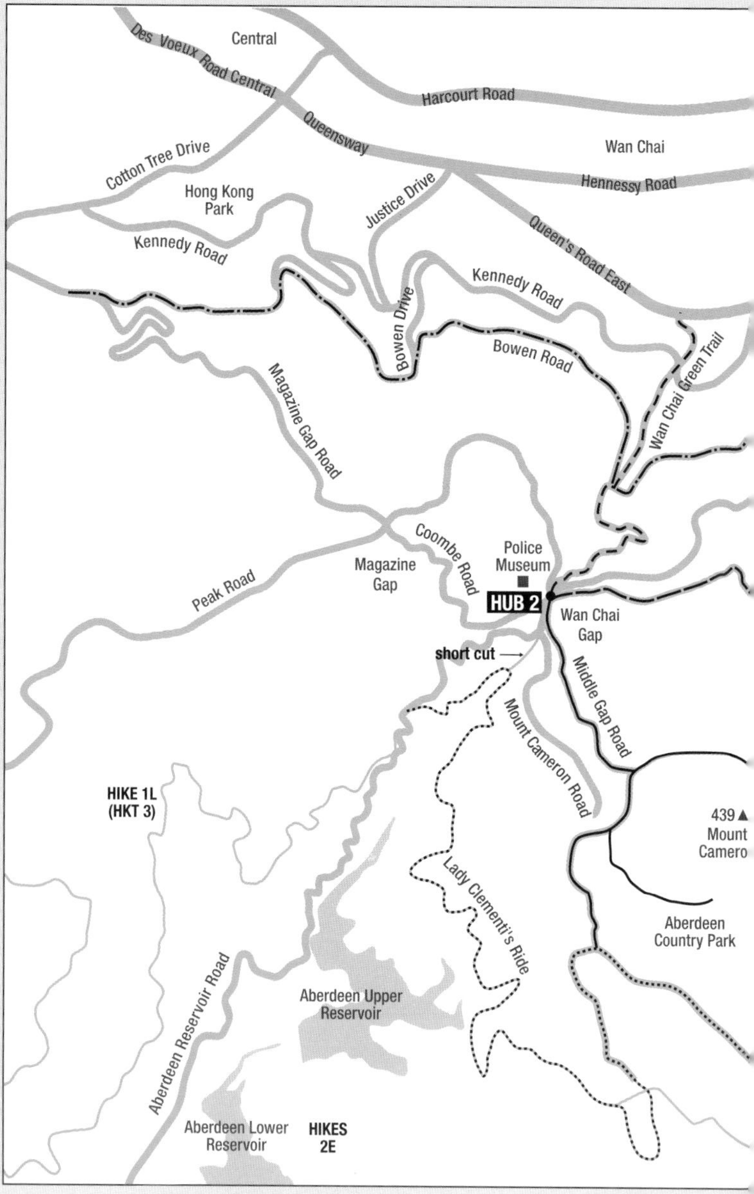

Map 2.1   2A   2B   2C   2D   2F

Central

Des Voeux Road Central

Harcourt Road

Queensway

Wan Chai

Cotton Tree Drive

Hennessy Road

Hong Kong Park

Justice Drive

Queen's Road East

Kennedy Road

Kennedy Road

Bowen Drive

Bowen Road

Wan Chai Green Trail

Magazine Gap Road

Coombe Road

Police Museum

HUB 2

Wan Chai Gap

Peak Road

Magazine Gap

short cut →

Middle Gap Road

Mount Cameron Road

HIKE 1L (HKT 3)

439 ▲ Mount Camero

Lady Clementi's Ride

Aberdeen Country Park

Aberdeen Reservoir Road

Aberdeen Upper Reservoir

Aberdeen Lower Reservoir

HIKES 2E

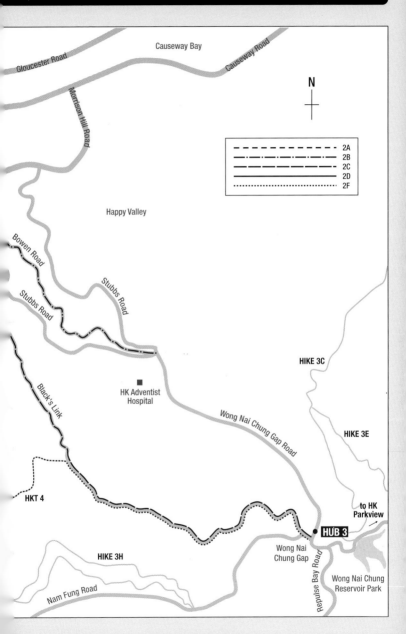

Causeway Bay

Gloucester Road

Causeway Road

Morrison Hill Road

N

2A
2B
2C
2D
2F

Happy Valley

Bowen Road

Stubbs Road

Stubbs Road

Black's Link

HK Adventist Hospital

HIKE 3C

Wong Nai Chung Gap Road

HIKE 3E

HKT 4

to HK Parkview

HUB 3

HIKE 3H

Wong Nai Chung Gap

Repulse Bay Road

Wong Nai Chung Reservoir Park

Nam Fung Road

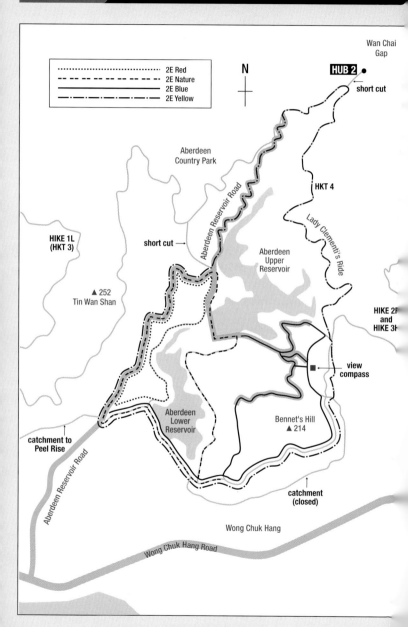

··········	2E Red
– – – – –	2E Nature
———	2E Blue
–·–·–·–	2E Yellow

N

Wan Chai Gap

HUB 2 ●

short cut

Aberdeen Country Park

HKT 4

Aberdeen Reservoir Road

Lady Clementi's Ride

short cut →

Aberdeen Upper Reservoir

HIKE 1L (HKT 3)

▲ 252 Tin Wan Shan

HIKE 2P and HIKE 3H

view compass

Aberdeen Lower Reservoir

Bennet's Hill ▲ 214

catchment to Peel Rise

Aberdeen Reservoir Road

catchment (closed)

Wong Chuk Hang

Wong Chuk Hang Road

A   WAN CHAI GAP ROAD AND WAN CHAI GAP GREEN TRAIL

N P

njoy a tree-shaded and quiet lane, only a few moments
n the crowded streets of the city. A very steep trail,
lded with informative markers about the plant life and
systems along the way, Wan Chai Gap Road is a good
to get to Bowen Road (Hike 2B). The transition from
gle to city (Queen's Road East, Wan Chai) is almost
abrupt. This is not a long road by itself, but can be
e as a round trip, or added to other walks to make
e very nice loops.

> Distance: 1.4 km/0.9 mi
> Difficulty: 3/5
> Time: 30 min
> Rise: 100 m
> 🧭 Map 2.1
> Countryside Map Grid:
> • Start and Finish:
>   08–09 and 65–66

To Get There

ting at Wan Chai Gap Park, stand at the intersection of Peak Road and Stubbs Road
h the park behind you. Wan Chai Gap Road is directly across Peak/Stubbs Road. The
l drops quickly out of sight.

There are some benches along the way and a sitting out area that is nicely shaded
ht at the beginning. The trail heads down the canyon and soon arrives at an
rsection, with CHOICES:

Wan Chai Gap Road — ahead

Bowen Road — left or right — see Hike 2B

Look for the Green Trail signs that identify various trees and plants and explain
ironmental issues as you travel down to the intersection with Kennedy Road and
re CHOICES:

**Wan Chai Gap Road — pick up the trail directly across Kennedy Road, but
you must briefly detour either left or right to get around the sidewalk rails
and cross the street.**

The Hopewell Center, where you could pick up a snack and take the elevators
down to Queen's Road East — left (west) up Kennedy Road

Bowen Road — left on Kennedy Road — Hike 2B

The last bit of trail passes a small park and the Pak Tai Temple, which is worth a look,
ore meeting Wan Chai Gap Road, then deposits you on Queen's Road East, just west of
nnedy Road. The old Wan Chai Post Office is to the left along Queen's Road East.

To Access the Trail from Wan Chai

On Queen's Road East, just before Stone Nullah Lane, go uphill on the lane alongside a small park and the temple. Turn right on Kennedy Road for a few meters, then cross the road to the Trail uphill on steps on the left.

ⒻⒹⓀⓈⓇⓍ

B BOWEN ROAD

rare Hong Kong hike: a flat paved trail. Winding in
out of the canyons above the city below, Bowen Road
ₙ to walk or run. There are fine views of the city and
ₙy small shrines along the way. There is also a fitness
rse.

Bowen Road is named after Sir George Bowen,
/ernor of Hong Kong from March 1883 to December
5.

> Distance: 4 km/2.5 mi
> Difficulty: 1/5
> Time: 45 min
> Rise: negligible
> 🧭 Map 2.1
> Countryside Map Grid:
> • Start: 09–10 and 65
> • Finish: 07–08 and 65–66

To Get There

can access the trail from Wan Chai Gap (Hike 2A), but most people will start it at
ᵣer end, so we have made an exception: instead of describing the trail from the Hub,
will describe Bowen Road from one end to the other.

Bus:

To the Stubbs Road (east) entrance, bus No. 6 from Central or No. 15 from Central
or the Peak
To the west entrance, minibus No. 1 from Star Ferry Pier

Foot:

To get to the center, take Wan Chai Gap Road, Hike 2A.
To get to the west entrance, walk up Cotton Tree Drive and go around the curve
above MacDonnell Road. Bowen Road is the fork to the left; the main street becomes
Magazine Gap Road. You could also walk down from the May Road Tramway stop.
It is not easy to walk to the east entrance, but you could get there from the end of
Black's Link (Hike 2C), Hong Kong Trail Section 4 (Hike 2F) or Hub 3 by walking
along Wong Nai Chung Gap Road to Stubbs Road.

Car:

ₜ very convenient. There is a tiny parking lot on Brewin Path across from the east
ₜrance to Bowen Road. There are a few metered spaces (2 hr) about half way up
ᵥen Drive, 17 at the intersection of Bowen Drive and Bowen Road, and 5 in front of
Bowen Road. You could park at Pacific Place and walk up from there (directions
ₒw). You also could park at the Hopewell Center and walk along Kennedy Road to
ₙ Chai Gap Road; see Hike 2A.

Starting at the Stubbs Road (east) entrance then, begin at roundabout just be
the Adventist Hospital. Bowen Road lies between the two wings of Stubbs Road ente
the circle, on the paved road. Walk onto the tree lined lane. Shortly, you pass a
Boundary Marker, dated 1903. The trail is marked every 500 meters. As you walk or
along, you pass fitness course exercise stations such as "Pull Up Bars," "Beam R
and a "Challenge Ladder" (what we used to call monkey bars). Happy Valley is on y
right and a waterfall dances down the hill on the left.

Near the 1,500-meter marker, for a sign that says "Lover's Stone Garden,"
steps up to Lover's Rock, also known as Amah's Rock. It is definitely worth the effo
see the many shrines and the quite suggestive rock, said to be a fertility shrine.

Continue on past an **emergency phone,** with signs indicating Shiu Fai Terrace
Stubbs Road) down the stairs and Wan Chai Gap Road straight ahead. Stairs also
down to a playground and volleyball court. These stairs extend beyond the ball c
and on down to Stubbs Road near the Sikh Temple (at Queen's Road East).

At the 2,000-meter marker you reach Wan Chai Gap Road, where you will
public toilets and a pocket park with a lovely bridge that crosses the stream. This is
half-way point and the end of the fitness course.

CHOICES:
* **Bowen Road — ahead**
* Wan Chai Gap Road to the Police Museum and Park — left — Hike 2A
* Wan Chai Gap Road to Queen's Road East and the Hopewell Center — righ
  Hike 2A

After you cross Borrett Road, traffic becomes more of a worry, but Bowen R
still remains flat. There is a pocket park on the left. By the 3500-meter marker, at Bo
Mansions, you have returned to the city, as Bowen Road becomes a two-lane traffic
road lined with high rise apartments.

The trail ends at Magazine Gap Road, just after the 4,000-meter marker (mar
"start" on the side of the marker facing Magazine Gap Road).

 To Continue to Hike
* Central Green Trail to Central — turn right at the sign for the Tramway Path
  Hike 1G.
* Chatham Path/Central Green Trail to the Peak — left — Hike 1G
* Along Magazine Gap Road to Robinson Road; then follow Robinson to Old P
  Road, taking it uphill to the Peak — ahead — Hike 1F
* As above, but continue on Robinson, to Kotewall Road and follow it to Hat
  Road, taking the Morning Trail and Cheung Po Tsai Path to the Peak — Hike

To Leave the Trail

Taxi/bus home.

Walk down Magazine Gap Road to Cotton Tree Road and from there visit to the Hong Kong Zoological and Botanical Gardens or continue down to Central.

riations

From Pacific Place, walk up Justice Drive past the British Consulate. Justice Drive peters out into a path, then becomes stairs; keep going up to Kennedy Road. Turn left on Kennedy Road. After a big curve, you will see Bowen Drive, a steep lane uphill to the right; take it to Bowen Road. About half way up Bowen Drive there are tennis courts, toilets and a few metered parking spaces.

You can also access Bowen Road via stairs from Shiu Fai Terrace or across from the Sikh Temple on Stubbs Road.

2C BLACK'S LINK

Ⓓ Ⓚ Ⓡ Ⓢ

As it gradually rises and falls, offering views of both sides of the Island, Black's Link offers a nice walk by itself or added on to other hikes. It's a good choice for runners. The road was named after Major General W. Black, General Officer commanding in Hong Kong in the late nineteenth century. He had the road built between Wong Nai Chung Gap and Magazine Gap, most likely in the late 1890s, to help get military troops to the Peak, where there were barracks and a hospital.

Distance: 3.2 km/2 mi
Difficulty: 2/5
Time: 1 hr
Rise: 50 m
Map 2.1
Countryside Map Grid:
• Start: 08–09 and 65–66
• Finish: 10–11 and 64

🚶 To Get There

Starting at Wan Chai Gap Park, stand at the intersection of Peak Road and Stubbs Road with the park behind you. Take Black's Link, the street gently sloping upward on the right.

The trail skirts the north side of Mount Cameron (439 m) for a mile or so (1.4 km) with peek-a-boo views of the harbor. At Middle Gap, right above Happy Valley (west side), the road levels off and the views widen. Now Black's Link gently descends to JUNCTION:

- **Wong Nai Chung Gap (Hong Kong Trail Section 4) — 1.8 km/1.1 mi; 40 min left**
- Wan Chai Gap — 1.4 km/0.9 mi; 30 min — back
- Aberdeen — 4 km/2.5 mi; 1 hr 10 min — right

There is an **emergency phone** at the junction. A covered bench sits here, oddly, there is not much to see. But just beyond this point, the trail slides along the south side of Mount Nicholson (430 m), with a spectacular series of views, encompassing Ocean Park, Aberdeen, Deep Water Bay and Lamma Island.

Note: The steep uphill road to the left leads to Black's Link Fresh Water Tank, a dead end.

The road now overlaps Hong Kong Trail Section 4; see Hike 2F. At marker H0 you can stop at a double picnic area. Follow the trail past the picnic tables for a better view to the south. The paved road heads gently down to marker H048, a JUNCTION and signboard:

Wong Nai Chung Gap — ahead
Nam Fung Road (Lady Clementi's Ride) — right down the stairs under the electric pylon — Hike 3H
Middle Gap (towards Wan Chai Gap) — back
o mileage is shown.)

Finally, at marker H049 a sign announces you are leaving Aberdeen Country Park. cend down the paved road, built up with apartments, which intersects with Deep er Bay Road, Repulse Bay Road, and Wong Nai Chung Gap Road.

To Continue to Hike
Hong Kong Trail Section 5, the Wilson Trail, and the entrance to Tai Tam Country Park are located on Tai Tam Reservoir Road just before Parkview; see Hub 3.
Return to Wan Chai Gap via Lady Clementi's Ride — retrace your steps to the signpost indicating the trail heading downhill; see Hike 3H.
Hong Kong Trail Section 4 — retrace your steps to the second junction, following signs; see Hike 2F.
Bowen Road — to make a nice loop, take Black's Link to Deep Water Bay Road turn left on Wan Nai Chung Gap Road and go down to Stubbs Road, where you can pick up Bowen Road; see Hike 2B.

To Leave the Trail
r left at the intersection on to Wong Nai Chung Gap Road:
Gas stations selling drinks/Order of St. John Memorial/Cricket Club
Bus or cab to Repulse Bay and eat at the rather upscale Spices (they have an outdoor patio) or Victoria City Seafood Restaurant at The Repulse Bay or at Tai Fat Hau, a seafood restaurant on the beach.
Up hill to the right to Parkview, with a grocery store and restaurants.
Bus stops for buses to Central or south side (cross the road to catch a bus to the south side)

2D MIDDLE GAP ROAD ®

Middle Gap Road is a good way to access several Wan Chai Gap hikes and runs. Open to cars, but lightly traveled, Middle Gap Road passes some unique homes. Our favorite is the mini Parthenon.

Distance: 2.3 km/1.4 mi
Difficulty: 2/5
Time: 30 min
Rise: negligible
Map 2.1
Countryside Map Grid:
• Start: 08–09 and 65–66
• Finish: 08–09 and 64–6

To Get There

Starting at Wan Chai Gap Park, stand at the intersection of Peak Road and Stubbs Road with the park behind you. Turn to the right and take the hill, Middle Gap Road, on the far side of Mount Cameron Road.

Walk up Middle Gap Road, starting with a pretty good climb, past the ama homes. After you start back downhill, two paths on the left climb into the woods, just before No. 15 and one at lamppost No. 36872 across from some tennis courts. I send you up about 250–275 steps to the top of Mount Cameron (439 m), under elec pylons. The first path has a right fork over an extremely pretty stream before the s begin. The views at the top are good, especially the second path, but marred by pylons. In a perfect world you would be able to go down the other side of M Cameron to Black's Link but you need your machete for that.

At the end of the road you come to a gate pole. Here the road turns into a pa lane. Follow the lane down. After a short time, you will come to a JUNCTION:

* **Aberdeen Reservoirs — 1.5 km/0.9 mi; 30 min — ahead — see Hike 2E**
* Black's Link via Hong Kong Trail Section 4 — 1.5 km/0.9 mi; 30 min — to the — a very nice loop back to Wan Chai Gap — Hike 2C
* Wan Chai Gap — 1 km/0.6 mi; 20 min — back

At the end of the lane, there is a traditional Chinese grave on the left, next modern electric pylon, which must give the dead a buzz.

To Continue to Hike

Further hiking is the only way to leave the trail

* Aberdeen Reservoir Road — right; see Hike 2E
* Lady Clementi's Ride — take the steps leading down next to the pylon and go or right; see Hike 3H.

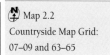

2E ABERDEEN COUNTRY PARK HIKES

Aberdeen Country Park is an especially fun area to wander around. Four clearly marked trails are described in detail below; you can also mix and match. The trails are good for kids, as the reservoirs provide lots to see. The park also contains the P.H.A.B. BBQ area, with tables adapted to the disabled and exercise equipment (and toilets) and a wheelchair hike. The Nature Trail identifies trees and plants along the trail. The Fitness Trail/Red Walk provides opportunities to increase your heart rate, such as pull ups and sit ups, and can be run. The Blue Walk has some demanding stairs, and treks up Bennet's Hill (214 m), with views to reward your effort. The Yellow Walk, the longest and most scenic, includes Lady Clementi's Ride. It circles the entire park and also takes you along the side of Bennet's Hill, with the option of climbing it.

> Map 2.2
> Countryside Map Grid:
> 07–09 and 63–65

To Get There

You can enter the park at Wan Chai Gap or at the Aberdeen Entrance. Because the hikes are drawn from the entrance we will describe them that way. Access via the Hub is described below.

On Foot:
Hong Kong Trail Section 2 or 3 (in reverse) — Hikes 1K, 1L

By Bus:
Aberdeen is a major bus and minibus interchange. From Central take bus No. 40; from Stanley take bus No. 73 or 973.

By Car:
Parking is available off Aberdeen Reservoir Road.

From the bus terminus, walk up Aberdeen Main Road (away from the harbor) then bear right on Aberdeen Reservoir Road up a big hill to the entrance to the Aberdeen Country Park. If you prefer you can take bus No. 7 or 76 or minibus No. 4C up the hill.

Brochures with detailed information are available at the Nature Centre, located at Aberdeen Management Centre, Aberdeen Country Park near the park entrance.

From the entrance, four hikes radiate through Aberdeen Country Park: the Fitness Trail (also called the Red Walk), the Nature Trail, the Blue Walk and the Yellow Walk. The colors for each hike are marked on the tip of direction signs, except for the Nature Trail which is marked with yellow markers low to the ground.

At the park entrance the SIGNPOST reads:

- Aberdeen — 0.5 km/0.3 mi; 15 min — back
- Aberdeen Upper Reservoir — 1.25 km/0.8 mi; 30 min — ahead
- Aberdeen Lower Reservoir — 0.25 km/0.1 mi; 15 min — right

Unhelpfully, both the ahead and right arrows are marked with red, blue and yellow tips.

FITNESS TRAIL/RED WALK — 2 km/1.25 mi; 1 hr — 13 exercise stations

From the entrance, take the right fork and follow the signs with red tips. At first the Red Walk overlaps the Blue and Yellow Walks. You pass two areas labeled "Morning Walker Garden," but they are simply small grassy areas with benches. On the left, a gate and steps are the back entrance of the Management Centre and the P.H.A.B. BBQ area. At the Lower Reservoir Dam, you come to a JUNCTION:

- **Aberdeen Upper Reservoir — 0.75 km/0.5 mi; 15 min — ahead — Red Walk**
- Aberdeen — 1 km/0.6 mi; 15 min — back — Blue, Red and Yellow Walks
- Aberdeen Nature Trail — right — across the dam you can see the Nature Trail Entrance Gate — this is also the way for the Blue and Yellow Walks.

One map board displays an Orienteering Course and another shows the Nature Trail.

The trail, dotted with exercise stations and BBQ sites, follows the side of the reservoir, and climbs a bit at the end when you reach the Upper Reservoir Dam (the last stairs themselves are included as fitness station No. 6). At the dam, the signs offer you CHOICES:

- **Wan Chai Gap — 1.75 km/1 mi; 45 min — left — Red and Blue Walks**
- To Lady Clementi's Ride — 0.75 km/0.5 mi; 15 min — right — Yellow Walk
- Aberdeen Lower Reservoir — 0.75 km/0.5 mi; 15 min — back

Separately a wooden sign shows "Fitness Trail — left."

The flat paved path, marked with nature signs and foot massage stations, cuts across a small spit of land through trees to the intersection with Aberdeen Reservoir Road at a JUNCTION:

- **Aberdeen Upper Reservoir — 0.25 km/0.1 mi; 15 min — left— Red, Blue and Yellow Walks**
- Wan Chai Gap — 1.75 km/1 mi; 45 min — ahead — Yellow Walk
- Aberdeen — 1.5 km/0.9 mi; 30 min — left — Red, Blue and Yellow Walks

Ahead, across the catchment, a small sign points up the stairs to the left:
- Hong Kong Trail — Watford Road — a short cut to the Hong Kong Trail Section 3, meeting it at marker H036; see Hike 1L.

Another sign shows the Fitness Trail to the left.

There are a map board, **emergency telephone,** and numerous BBQ areas.

After passing fitness station No. 12, near the end, the catchwater veers off to the right. A signpost shows:
- **Aberdeen — 1 km/0.6 mi; 15 min — ahead**
- Aberdeen Upper Reservoir — 0.75 km/0.5 mi; 15 min — back
- unmarked — the catchwater continues about 1.5 km/0.9 mi; 15 min to Peel Rise; see Hike 1L

Keep going down the road to return to the entrance.

ATURE TRAIL — 1.2 km/0.75 mi; 50 minutes — 20 stops

ote: 50 minutes is a generous time estimate for this walk unless you are a slow reader.

The Nature Trail is marked with yellow arrow-shaped signposts that are low to the round (not to be confused with the Yellow Walk, which is designated with a yellow ripe at the tip of the arrow signs, about 6 feet above ground).

From the entrance, take the right fork and follow the signs with red tips, following e overlapping Red, Yellow and Blue Walks. At the Lower Reservoir Dam, you come to JUNCTION:

- **Aberdeen Nature Trail — right — across the dam you can see the Nature Trail entrance gate — this is also the way for the Blue and Yellow Walks.**
  Aberdeen Upper Reservoir — 0.75 km/0.5 mi; 15 min — ahead — Red Walk
  Aberdeen — 1 km/0.6 mi; 15 min — back — Blue, Red and Yellow Walks

Crossing over the dam and through the entrance gate, you will immediately see a ap of the Nature Trail and the first of the 20 signs. When the trail splits, **take the right rk up the steps** (the left fork goes to a BBQ site).

Crest the steps to find a nifty view of Aberdeen Harbor, looking down on the mbo Floating Restaurant and the Chinese style Roman Catholic Seminary, with Ap

Lei Chau behind. Then enter the woods, curving downhill to a catchwater. **The low yellow arrow points your way to the Nature Trail up about 25 stairs to the left.** (When we were last by, a sign showed the catchwater was closed. If open, it would intersect with Lady Clementi's Ride, Hike 3H.)

At a fork in the steps, a signpost shows:

- **Aberdeen Upper Reservoir — 1 km/0.6 mi; 30 min — left**
- Lady Clementi's Ride — 1.25 km/0.8 mi; 30 min — ahead — Blue and Yellow Walks
- Aberdeen Lower Reservoir — 0.25 km/0.1 mi; 10 min — back — Blue and Yellow Walks

Low yellow arrows point back and left.

The pleasant trail, rock and concrete paved and generally flat or gently sloping up and down, follows the east side of the Lower Reservoir; there are few views but specific trees and plants, sights and sounds are noted on signs along the way. An old gravesite by an iron fern marker is ignored. At an electric pylon, steps to the right lead to a BBQ site, then up a steep hill to the Blue Walk. Even the pylon is posted with questions about appropriate ways to care for the environment. After passing BBQ site 4, about 5 stairs take you up to a JUNCTION:

- **Aberdeen Upper Reservoir — 0.25 km/0.1 mi; 15 min — left**
- Lady Clementi's Ride — 0.5 km/0.3 mi; 15 min — right — nature signs continue and the trail meets the Blue Walk at the map board
- Aberdeen Nature Trail — back

A very old rain gauge (Tien Fa Dan) located behind a metal fence in the middle BBQ site 3 is worth a look.

Almost immediately, you reach a map board and the Upper Reservoir Dam. Cross the dam, and the walk rejoins Aberdeen Reservoir Road at its junction with the Blue, Red and Yellow Walks. See end of Fitness Trail above. Turn left to return to the start.

BLUE WALK — 3.8 km/2.4 mi; 2 hours

From the entrance, take the right fork and follow the signs with red tips. At first the Blue Walk overlaps the Red and Yellow Walks. At the Lower Reservoir Dam, see JUNCTION:

- **Aberdeen Nature Trail — right — this is also the way for the Yellow Walk**
- Aberdeen Upper Reservoir — 0.75 km/0.5 mi; 15 min — ahead — Red Walk
- Aberdeen — 1 km/0.6 mi; 15 min — back — Blue, Red and Yellow Walks

Turn right and cross over the dam, under the entrance gate for the Nature Trail. Follow the Nature Trail as above to the first JUNCTION at the fork on the steps:

- **Lady Clementi's Ride — 1.25 km/0.8 mi; 30 min — ahead — Blue Walk**
- Aberdeen Upper Reservoir — 1 km/0.6 mi; 30 min — left (Nature Trail)
- Aberdeen Lower Reservoir — 0.25 km/0.1 mi; 10 min — back — Blue Walk

Low yellow Nature Trail arrows point back and left.

Be prepared! There are more than 200 steep steps up the hill. At the top of the steps, wonderful views stretch to the south and include all of Aberdeen. Enjoy your reward, a priceless view of Aberdeen Harbor, the Roman Catholic Seminary, the Jumbo Floating Restaurant, the bridge to Ap Lei Chau, the shipping channel and over to Lamma Island. You now have some CHOICES:

- **Aberdeen Upper Reservoir — 1.25 km/0.75 mi; 30 min — left — Blue Walk**
- Aberdeen Lower Reservoir — 0.5 km/0.3 mi; 15 min — back — Blue and Yellow Walks
- Lady Clementi's Ride — 1 km/0.6 mi; 15 min — right — Yellow Walk, and Yellow Walk to Blue Walk

You will find a rocky, but flat dirt path with occasional views; trees provide welcome shade. About 5 minutes, the trail connects to a concrete road which winds in and out along the hillside and through some tree covered sections. You arrive at a signpost and some CHOICES:

- **Aberdeen Upper Reservoir — 1 km/0.6 mi; 15 min — right — Blue Walk**
- Aberdeen Lower Reservoir — 0.75 km/0.5 mi; 15 min — or Lady Clementi's Ride — 1.5 km/0.9 mi; 30 min — back — Blue Walk
- BBQ or Aberdeen Nature Trail — a path down to the left leads down a steep hill to BBQ site 5 and connects to the Nature Trail at an electric pylon and a sign — Aberdeen Lower Reservoir (left) Aberdeen Upper Reservoir (right). No time or distance given but it is about 10 minutes.

The walk travels a concrete path with views of Mount Nicholson ahead. A paved road cutting sharply back to the left leads only to an electric pylon. Ignore it and press on to a JUNCTION:

Aberdeen Upper Reservoir — 0.75 km/0.5 mi; 15 min — ahead — no tip marks
Lady Clementi's Ride — 0.25 km/0.1 mi; 15 min — right — Blue Walk. Stairs take you up to the top of Bennet's Hill (214 m) where a view compass identifies the many sights of Aberdeen.
Aberdeen Lower Reservoir — 1.25 km/0.8 mi; 30 min — back

Although the Blue Walk is signed to the right, chose the route ahead to meet it on the north side of Bennet's Hill. The path ahead leads to another opportunity to climb Bennet's Hill at a JUNCTION:

- **Aberdeen Upper Reservoir — 0.25 km/0.1 mi; 15 min — ahead**
- View compass — right
- Aberdeen Lower Reservoir — 1.25 km/0.8 mi; 30 min — back

Again you can go right to meet the Blue Walk or ahead to meet it on the far side of Bennet's Hill. We stick to the trail and in just a few meters reach another JUNCTION:

- **Lady Clementi's Ride — 0.5 km/0.3 mi; 15 min — right**
- Aberdeen Upper Reservoir — 0.25 km/0.1 mi; 15 min — left — the road takes you to the Upper Reservoir Dam. Enroute you can pick up the Nature Trail or cross the dam to Aberdeen Reservoir Road and the Fitness Trail/Red Walk
- Aberdeen Lower Reservoir — 1.25 km/0.8 mi; 30 min — back

There is a map board here.

Resisting the temptation to cut out here, take the road about 0.5 km to the right to the JUNCTION of the Blue Walk, Yellow Walk, and Lady Clementi's Ride:

- **To Aberdeen Lower Reservoir via Bennet's Hill — 1.5 km/0.9 mi; 30 min — right — Blue Walk**
- To Black's Link via Middle Gap Road — 3.25 km/2 mi; 1 hr — ahead — this also takes you to the Yellow Walk along the side of Bennet's Hill and back to the park entrance.
- Wan Chai Gap — 2.25 km/1.4 mi; 45 min — left — Yellow Walk
- Aberdeen Upper Reservoir — 1 km/0.6 mi; 15 min — back — Blue Walk

Tree Walk signs begin here, and there is a covered viewing pavilion and picnic area.

You've avoided the climb twice, you can't put it off any longer and the view really is a full recompense for the effort. (However, we have to admit that you can get almost as a good a view by taking the Yellow Walk along the hillside. Go ahead a bit downhill to a second junction at the foot of an electric pylon, then right along the Yellow Walk. It takes about 135 steps to get to the top, where you have several alternative trails down:

- **Aberdeen Lower Reservoir — 1.25 km/0.8 mi; 30 min — ahead, around the pylon**
- Aberdeen Upper Reservoir — 0.5 km/0.3 mi; 15 min — right — this takes you the view compass intersection you passed earlier. You could take it down and then take the shortcut to the Nature Trail or cross the dam to the Fitness Trail/Red Walk.
- Lady Clementi's Ride — 0.25 km/0.1 mi; 15 min — back — Blue Walk

The trail is dirt and rather flat, passing a picnic table to a panorama map on the left. The Island lies before you from Mount Cameron (439 m) to the Twins (363 and 386 m) and Middle Bay.

Descend about 50 steps to a JUNCTION:

- **Middle Gap or Nam Fung Road — (no distance noted) — ahead — odd signage, as the quickest way to Middle Gap or Nam Fung Road is back the way you came.**
- Aberdeen Reservoir — right — steps down to the Blue Walk
- To Wan Chai Gap via Lady Clementi's Ride — 2.5 km/1.6 mi; 1 hr — back

About 75 more steps down, facing a splendid view, there is yet another JUNCTION:

- **Aberdeen Lower Reservoir — 1.25 km/0.8 mi; 30 min — right — Yellow Walk**
- Middle Gap or Nam Fung Road — (no distance noted but it is perhaps 3.0 km/ 1.8 mi; 1 hr to Nam Fung Road) — left — Yellow Walk
- Aberdeen Upper Reservoir — 0.75 km/0.5 mi; 15 min — back

The Blue Walk now overlaps the Yellow, along a rocky dirt path with terrific views over the Aberdeen Sports Ground, Shouson Hill and Repulse Bay, then curving around Bennet's Hill, the harbor and shipping channel. The trail returns you to the intersection of the Blue and Yellow Walks by the rock face at top of the steps:

- **Aberdeen Lower Reservoir — 0.5 km/0.3 mi; 15 min — left — Blue Walk**
- Aberdeen Upper Reservoir — 1.25 km/0.75 mi; 30 min — ahead — Blue Walk
- Lady Clementi's Ride — 1 km/0.6 mi; 15 min — back — Yellow and Blue Walks

Descend some steep steps and turn right at the catchment, as the trail takes you back to the Lower Reservoir Dam, which you cross to reach the park entrance.

YELLOW WALK — 5.9 km/3.7 mi; 3 hr

The Yellow Walk has one section filled with spectacular views; the rest, like the other walks in Aberdeen Country Park, is leafy and wooded.

Follow the directions for the Blue Walk up to the third JUNCTION at the top of the 200 steps:

- **Lady Clementi's Ride — 1 km/0.6 mi; 15 min — right — Yellow Walk**
- Aberdeen Upper Reservoir — 1.25 km/0.75 mi; 30 min — left —Blue Walk
- Aberdeen Lower Reservoir — 0.5 km/0.3 mi; 15 min — back — Blue and Yellow Walks

Clamber across the rocky outcropping and follow the rocky dirt trail east. Deep Water Bay and Middle Island will be in your panoramic view. Here the trail is very open and exposed, mostly flat, with some ups and downs. Some sections are quite rocky. Curving around Bennet's Hill, and a new display of views, the trail meets the Blue Walk at a JUNCTION:

- **Middle Gap or Nam Fung Road — (no distance noted, but it is about 3 km, 1.8 mi; 1 hr) — ahead — Yellow Walk**
- Aberdeen Upper Reservoir — 0.75 km/0.5 mi; 15 min — left — Blue Walk
- Aberdeen Lower Reservoir — 1.25 km/0.8 mi; 30 min — back — Yellow Walk

Enjoy the views for they soon disappear into shrubbery as the trail meets catchwater. An arrow low to the ground points left and the signpost is above you on the left:

- **Aberdeen Upper Reservoir or Wan Chai Gap — left (no distance noted, see second junction)**
- To Black's Link via Middle Gap Road — 3.25 km/2 mi; 1 hr — right
- To Nam Fung Road via Lady Clementi's Ride — 2.75 km/1.7 mi; 45 min — right
- Aberdeen Lower Reservoir — 1.5 km/0.9 mi; 30 min — back

Turn left and go up the stairs then left again to a second JUNCTION:

- **Wan Chai Gap — 2.25 km/1.4 mi; 45 min — right — Yellow Walk**
- To Black's Link via Middle Gap Road — 3.25 km/2 mi; 1 hr — behind you
- Aberdeen Upper Reservoir — 1 km/0.6 mi; 15 min — left — Blue Walk
- To Aberdeen Lower Reservoir via Bennet's Hill — 1.5 km/0.9 mi; 30 min — straight ahead — Blue Walk

The Yellow Walk follows Lady Clementi's Ride, which is also the Hong Kong Trail Section 4 and a Tree Walk (see Hikes 2F and 3H), for a couple of kilometers to a JUNCTION:

- **Peel Rise to Wan Chai Gap (Hong Kong Trail Section 3) — 5.75 km/3.5 mi; 1 hr 45 min — ahead — Yellow Walk and Hike 1L**
- Wan Chai Gap — 0.25 km/0.1 mi; 5 min — right and up. This is a shortcut to Aberdeen Reservoir Road, and worth considering if you are planning to go up to Wan Chai Gap
- Black's Link via Middle Gap Road (Hong Kong Trail Section 4) — 5 km/3.2 mi; 1 hr 30 min — back — Yellow Walk

At the intersection with Aberdeen Reservoir Road a JUNCTION:

- **Aberdeen Upper Reservoir — 1.2 km/0.8 mi; 20 min — left**
- Morning Walkers' Garden — worth a detour — a delightful little place with marigolds, hibiscus, dahlia, shrubs, and a little sitting out area — across the road

The first path is unmarked, the second is signed: either path works as they both circle back to Aberdeen Reservoir Road.

- Peel Rise to Wan Chai Gap (Hong Kong Trail Section 3) — 5.5 km/3.5 mi; 1 hr 40 min — left across the bridge and right up the stairs — Hike 1L
- Wan Chai Gap — 0.6 km/0.4 mi; 15 min — right
- To Black's Link via Lady Clementi's Ride and Middle Gap Road (Hong Kong Trail Section 4) — 5.56 km/3.5 mi; 1 hr 40 min — back

Note the large trunk fig tree on the right; the fruit grows on the trunk.

Aberdeen Reservoir Road s-curves its way down the hill, steep in some spots, crossing over a few streams. There are several benches.

As you reach the Upper Reservoir you first see remnants of World War II buildings on the left side of the road, then a picnic area on the right with sheltered benches, then the junction of Aberdeen Reservoir Road with the four trails. From here, the Yellow Walk overlaps the Fitness Trail/Red Walk; see above.

Alternatives

For a good running loop, take the Blue Walk (the stairs are a fine warm-up) to the Upper Reservoir Dam and then back to the park entrance on the Fitness Trail/Red Walk, about 3 km/1.9 mi. If that's not enough, you could add in the Lady Clementi's loop for another 4.4 km/2.75 mi; see Hike 3H. Or you could add in the catchwater to Peel Rise, about 1.5 km/0.9 mi each way. See end of Red Walk, above.

Access the Trail from Wan Chai Gap

Starting at Wan Chai Gap Park, stand at the intersection of Peak Road and Stubbs Road with the park behind you. Turn to the right and take flat Mount Cameron Road along the side of the park for a short distance until you come to the water department building on the right. Aberdeen Reservoir Road winds downhill, just in front of the building, next to the sign for Aberdeen Country Park. Follow Aberdeen Reservoir Road about 9 minutes, to a signboard noting the four paths:

Aberdeen — 1.5 km/0.9 mi; 30 min — right — Fitness Trail/Red Walk, Blue Walk
Aberdeen Upper Reservoir — 0.22 km/0.1 mi; 5 min — Nature Trail, Yellow Walk — straight ahead over the dam
Wan Chai Gap — 1.7 km/1 mi; 45 min — back

There is a BBQ site to the left. **There is also an emergency phone**.

The map at the head of Aberdeen Reservoir Road, at Wan Chai Gap, is marked with the Red, Blue and Yellow Walks.

2F HONG KONG TRAIL SECTION 4 — WAN CHAI GAP to WONG NAI CHUNG GAP

You will enjoy beautiful south side views all along this trail, but beware, it is a more challenging trail than some maps suggest, as you climb up and down a fair amount. About mid-way, there is a sheltered picnic spot with especially good views, a perfect place to stop for lunch. There are lengthy flat parts that are good for running, interspersed with stairs. The trail includes a Tree Walk and follows part of Lady Clementi's Ride; see Hike 3H.

> Distance: 7.5 km/4.7 mi
> Difficulty: 2/5
> Time: 2 hr
> Rise: 200 m
> Maps 2.2 and 2.3
> Countryside Map Grid:
> • Start: 08–09 and 65–66
> • Finish: 10–11 and 64

To Get There

Starting at Wan Chai Gap Park, stand at the intersection of Peak Road and Stubbs Roa with the park behind you. Turn to the right and take flat Mount Cameron Road alon the side of the park for a short distance until you come to the water department buildi on the right.

Aberdeen Reservoir Road winds downhill, just in front of the building, next to t sign for Aberdeen Country Park. Quite soon, you will arrive at a sign for Lady Clemen Ride and a signposted JUNCTION:

- **Aberdeen Upper Reservoir — 1.5 km/0.9 mi; 30 min — straight — the si has the Yellow Walk tips; see Hike 2E**
- Black's Link via Lady Clementi's Ride and Magazine Gap Road — 5.25 km/3.3 r 1 hr 30 min — left fork downhill. This is a shortcut to Hong Kong Trail Section joining it between H038 and H039.
- Wan Chai Gap — 0.25 km/0.1 mi; 15 min (the time is exaggerated, perhaps beca the road is steep uphill)— back

Proceed down to just before the bridge and the signpost for the Hong Kong Tr CHOICES:

- **To Black's Link via Lady Clementi's Ride and Middle Gap Road (Hong Kc Trail Section 4) — 5.56 km/3.5 mi; 1 hr 40 min — left before the bridge**
- Morning Walkers' Garden — worth a detour — a delightful place with marigo hibiscus, dahlia, shrubs, and a little sitting out area — right. The first righ unmarked, the second right is signed: either path works as they both circle bac Aberdeen Reservoir Road.

- Peel Rise to Wan Chai Gap (Hong Kong Trail Section 3) — 5.5 km/3.5 mi; 1 hr 40 min — across the bridge and right up the stairs — Hike 1L
- Aberdeen Upper Reservoir — 1.16 km/0.75 mi; 20 min — straight
- Wan Chai Gap — 0.62 km/0.4 mi; 15 min — back

The flat dirt trail, interspersed with stairs, leads into the woods, passing several pretty stream beds; unfortunately, many are marred by ugly water drainage pipes. Watch for the Tree Walk markers identifying native plants, among them an Incense Tree, for which Hong Kong ("Fragrant Harbor") is believed to be named.

Climb a short flight of stairs to the next JUNCTION:

- **Black's Link via Middle Gap Road (Hong Kong Trail Section 4) — 5 km/3.2 mi; 1 hr 30 min — ahead. This marker bears the yellow tips of the Aberdeen Yellow Walk; see Hike 2E.**
- Wan Chai Gap — 0.25 km/0.1 mi; 15 min (the time is exaggerated, perhaps because the trail is uphill) — left and up
- Peel Rise to Wan Chai Gap (Hong Kong Trail Section 3) — 5.75 km/3.5 mi; 1 hr 45 min — back

Continuing downhill along the path, passing a waterfall and crossing a stone bridge, you will get occasional views of Mount Kellett (501 m). The trail remains mostly level. After marker H040, a signpost appears, although there is no obvious junction; perhaps is to orient you if you stop for a break at the little picnic spot nearby.

Wan Chai Gap — 1.25 km/0.8 mi; 30 min — ahead

Black's Link via Middle Gap Road — 4.25 km/2.6 mi; 1 hr 15 min — back

Both directions bear Yellow Walk tips; see Aberdeen Country Park Hikes, Hike 2E.

Pass more Tree Walk markers and streambeds as you travel on towards Black's nk. After you cross a second stone bridge, you can detour up stairs to the left to a orld War II bunker. Just down the trail on the left, there is a pretty picnic spot, where you can admire the view, which includes Brick Hill, Ocean Park, the driving school, ddle Island and Repulse Bay. But don't stop for long here, more views await you, as ll as shaded tables.

Go down the long flight of steps, then stairs, and cross over the catchwater — with limpse of the reservoir. Then step up to a well-manicured picnic spot, with tables d a roofed patio. The area is ringed with native flowers and affords a stupendous view the south side of Hong Kong, from Repulse Bay to Aberdeen. Here you will find a ble JUNCTION, as you have reached the intersection of the Blue and Yellow Walks Aberdeen Country Park; see Hike 2E:

First:
- **To Black's Link via Middle Gap Road — 3.25 km/2 mi; 1 hr — left**
- Aberdeen Upper Reservoir — 1 km/0.6 mi; 15 min — right — Hike 2E (Walk)
- Aberdeen Lower Reservoir via Bennet's Hill — 1.5 km/0.9 mi; 30 min — straight ahead — Hike 2E (Blue Walk)
- Wan Chai Gap — 2.25 km/1.4 mi; 45 min — back — Hike 2E (Yellow Walk)

Second (down the hill to the left):
- **To Black's Link via Middle Gap Road — 3.25 km/2 mi; 1 hr — ahead**
- To Nam Fung Road via Lady Clementi's Ride — 2.75 km/1.7 mi; 45 min — ah
- Aberdeen Lower Reservoir — 1.5 km/0.9 mi; 30 min — down steps to the righ Hike 2E (Blue Walk)
- Aberdeen Upper Reservoir or Wan Chai Gap — back (no distance noted, see al junction) — Hike 2E (Yellow Walk)

The tree markers end here.

The flat path follows the catchwater, but wanders away from it a couple of time go around hills. At marker H043, there is a lovely grove of trees and vines. You can you're not too far from civilization as you hear the roar of cars below. Mount Came (439 m) rises above you. You come to another JUNCTION:
- **Black's Link via Middle Gap Road (Hong Kong Trail Section 4) — 2.25 1.4 mi; 1 hr — left up the stairs**
- Nam Fung Road via Lady Clementi's Ride — 1.75 km/1 mi; 30 min — strai, continuing along the catchwater
- Aberdeen Reservoir (Hong Kong Trail Section 4) — 0.5 km/0.3 mi; 1 hr 45 mir back (the time is inconsistent with the distance, and should be 15 mins; it is al 45 min to either reservoir)

Climb the many steps to your left, and stop for breath with the excuse that you examining the old, but still maintained, Chinese gravesite. Looking back over the cc you can now see both sides of Brick Hill and the Aberdeen Harbor. You have begu climb up Mount Cameron, passing H044 as you mount a paved lane to a JUNCTIC
- **Black's Link via Hong Kong Trail Section 4 — 1.5 km/0.9 mi; 30 min — rig**
- Wan Chai Gap — 1 km/0.6 mi; 15 min — ahead
- Aberdeen Reservoirs — 1.5 km/0.9 mi; 30 min — back

Go right along a wide and rather flat paved lane with a curb on the right and hill on your left for one of the best views of the trail. Soon you will enjoy a 180-deg

v of the south side, including Aberdeen, Brick Hill (284 m), Bennet's Hill (214 m),
ung Hom Kok with the Hong Kong Jockey Club Cheshire Home on the end, Violet
(433 m) and Stanley Peninsula, and you can look back and see the Blue and Yellow
rdeen Park hikes up Bennet's Hill out of Aberdeen Country Park; see Hike 2E.

Good views continue for the next kilometer or so. After H045, round the curve for
ther super view. At an unnumbered Hong Kong Trail marker, the pavement ends
the trail becomes a gentle uphill mix of stone steps and a dirt path. As the trail
ds away from the water, open areas alternate with covered ones.

Enjoy another good view at marker H046, then the path becomes increasingly
oded with fewer, but nevertheless excellent, views until you go up a few stairs and
rge at a JUNCTION with a paved road, Black's Link, and a covered rest stop:

Wong Nai Chung Gap — 1.8 km/1.1 mi; 40 min — right

Wan Chai Gap — 1.4 km/0.9 mi; 30 min — left

Aberdeen — 4 km/2.5 mi; 1 hr 10 min — back

There is an **emergency phone** and a shelter with Government posters at this point.
Take a well-deserved break in the shade and then proceed down the road to the
it. (Ignore the paved road up to the left; it dead ends at the Black's Link Fresh Water
ervoir Tank.) You can look down to the right and see Wong Nai Chung Gap Road as
es through the Aberdeen Tunnel; just beyond, you can see the Ocean Park seahorse
he hill.

Reaching marker H047, you will find a double picnic area: follow the trail past the
nic spot for a good view. Across the way, steps up to the left provide a detour for
re views. The paved road heads gently down to a JUNCTION, marker H048, and a
iboard (no mileage is listed):

Wong Nai Chung Gap — ahead

Nam Fung Road (Lady Clementi's Ride) — right down the stairs under the electric
pylon; see Hike 3H

Middle Gap (towards Wan Chai Gap) — back

Finally, at marker H049, a sign announces you are leaving Aberdeen Country Park.
cend to the bottom of the paved road, which intersects with Deep Water Bay Road,
ulse Bay Road, and Wong Nai Chung Gap Road.

To Continue to Hike

Hong Kong Trail Section 5 (Hike 3A), the Wilson Trail (Hikes 3B and 3F), and the
entrance to Tai Tam Country Park (Hikes 3D and 3E) are located on Tai Tam
Reservoir Road just before Parkview; see Hub 3.

- Return to Wan Chai Gap via Lady Clementi's Ride — Retrace your steps to the signpost indicating the trail heading downhill; see Hike 3H.
- Bowen Road — to make a loop, take Deep Water Bay Road to Wan Nai Chung Gap Road, and go left down to Stubbs Road; see Hike 2B.

To Leave the Trail

Bear left at the intersection onto Wong Nai Chung Gap Road. You'll find:

- Gas stations selling drinks
- Bus or cab to Repulse Bay and eat at the rather upscale Spices (they have an outdoor patio) or Victoria City Seafood at Repulse Bay or at Tai Fat Hau, a seafood restaurant on the beach.
- Bus stops for buses to Central or south side (cross the road to catch a bus to the south side)

Go up the hill to the right on Tai Tam Reservoir Road for Parkview, a large apartment development with a grocery store and restaurants.

WONG NAI CHUNG GAP

/ong Nai Chung Gap is full of hiking opportunities in Tai Tam Country Park,
cially for hikers looking for challenges and spectacular views. This Hub has it all:
ks, reservoirs, splendid views, and stairs, stairs, stairs. Your sore muscles may not
k you, but your mirror will. There are some gentle hikes too.

Map 3.1 and 3.2

ntryside Map Grid: 10–11 and 64

To Get There

Bus:

No. 6 or 66 from Central and from Stanley. Get off at the gas station at the crest of
hill. If your chosen hike starts at Parkview you will have to walk up Tai Tam Reservoir
d, a workout in itself.

Foot:

From Hong Kong Trail Section 4 and Black's Link — left on Wong Nai Chung Gap
Road and right, if need be, up Tai Tam Reservoir Road; see Hike 2F.

East along Bowen Road and then up Wong Nai Chung Gap Road and left, if need
be, up Tai Tam Reservoir Road; see Hike 2B.

Tai Tam Reservoir Road from the Tai Tam County Park entrance on Tai Tam Road.
See Countryside Map Grid 13–14 and 62.

Car:

xpensive parking is available at the foot of Tai Tam Reservoir Road. The lot is on the
just after you turn up the road. There are a few spaces on the left just before the
rance to Parkview and expensive parking in Parkview (cheaper if you go for a big
cery shop after your hike).

3A HONG KONG TRAIL SECTION 5 (MOUNT BUTLER) — WONG NAI CHUNG GAP TO MOUNT PARKER ROAD 🄢 🄟 🄢

A very challenging hike, and in return very rewarding, this trail undulates over the hills from Parkview to Quarry Gap, cresting Mount Butler (436 m). There are numerous steps, both up and down; many of them are quite steep and awkward in dimension. However, the climb is well worth the effort for the fabulous vistas in all directions.

Distance: 4 km/2.5 mi	Difficulty: 5/5	Time: 1 hr 30 min
Rise: 130 m	Map 3.1	
Countryside Map Grid: • Start: 11–12 and 64 • Finish: 12–13 and 65		

3B WILSON TRAIL SECTION 2 — PARKVIEW TO QUARRY BAY 🄝 🄢 🄟 🄢

The views on this trail are some of the best on the Island, and are a fair reward for the sweat to get there. Initially, the trail climbs up along Hong Kong Trail Section (Hike 3A), then turns along the Wilson Trail for another uphill section, before many sections of seriously steep steps downhill. Towards the end, the trail becomes a Tree Walk that includes World War II ruins, and finally ends in Tai Koo Shing. A good challenge!

Distance: 6.6 km/4.1 mi	Difficulty: 5/5	Time: 2 hr 30 min
Rise: 230 m	Map 3.1	
Countryside Map Grid: • Start: 11–12 and 64 • Finish: 13 and 67		

3C SIR CECIL'S RIDE 🄚 🄝 🄡 🄢

Sir Cecil's Ride offers broad views of the harbor from a fairly level path, with some colorful rest stops and shrines tucked into the forest along the way. After a brief steep uphill on paved roads, the path takes a flat meandering course towards Braemar Hill (200 m). Finally, the trail connects with the flat Quarry Bay Jogging Trail and ends in Quarry Bay. A classic Hong Kong hike in the countryside, just barely above the city.

Distance: 8.9 km/5.6 mi	Difficulty: 2/5	Time: 3 hr
Rise: negligible	Map 3.1	
Countryside Map Grid: • Start: 10–11 and 64 • Finish: 12–13 and 66		

3D TAI TAM RESERVOIR COUNTRY PARK LOOP 🄓 🄚 🄝 🄡 🄢

Circling the Intermediate Reservoir, the loop offers the scenic parts of Tai Tam Reservoir Road and a pretty ramble through the woods. A bit long but not very difficult, kids might enjoy this one, especially the Lower Path section, which requires some rock scrambling. The road itself is a pleasant hike, which many people do with kids or strollers. Except for a little bump at the beginning, it is all down one way and all up the other, so don't underestimate the energy you will need to get back uphill.

Distance: 6 km/3.8 mi	Difficulty: 2/5	Time: 2 hr
Rise: 300 m	Map 3.2	
Countryside Map Grid: • Start and Finish: 11–12 and 64		
Repulse Bay Gap is just northwest of 12 and 62. Tai Tam Reservoir Road meets Tai Tam Road at 13–14 and 62.		

E TAI TAM COUNTRY TRAIL 🅝 🆂

An excellent walk that mixes flat and hilly sections, each with its own feel. The loop combines some of the best features of the trails in Hub 3. It is not quite as difficult as the hardest trails but nonetheless has some of those not-to-be-missed views.

Distance: 5.2 km/3.3 mi	Difficulty: 4/5	Time: 2 hr 30 min
Rise: 100 m	Map 3.2	
Countryside Map Grid: • Start and Finish: 11–12 and 64		
The loop extends from 10–11 and 64–65 to 11–12 and 63.		

F WILSON TRAIL SECTION 1 — VIOLET HILL AND THE TWINS 🆂 🅟 🆂

This hike heads south from Parkview over Violet Hill (433 m), which affords almost 360-degree views. Then on to one of the most challenging hikes on Hong Kong Island, more than 1,000 steps that give even the hardiest pause as the trail mounts the Twins (363 m and 386 m). But the views are grand and there is a well-earned sense of accomplishment when you finish.

Distance: 4.8 km/3 mi	Difficulty: 5/5	Time: 2 hr
Rise: 386 m	Map 3.2 and 3.3	
Countryside Map Grid: • Start: 11–12 and 64 • Finish: 12–13 and 60–61		

G TSZ LO LAN SHAN PATH AND CATCHWATER TO STANLEY 🆁

An alternative and gentler route from Parkview to Repulse Bay Gap. A good part of the trail is a concrete catchwater, which could be run. It is tempting to recommend this hike for kids, as it is flat, but in many areas there is a steep drop off so any children should be firmly attached to an adult.

Distance: 6 km/3.8 mi	Difficulty: 1/5	Time: 1 hr 30 min
Rise: negligible	Map 3.2 and 3.3	
Countryside Map Grid: • Start: 11 and 64 • Finish: 12–13 and 60–61		
Repulse Bay Gap is just northwest of 12 and 62.		

3H   LADY CLEMENTI'S RIDE Ⓚ Ⓝ Ⓡ

A lot of variety, good but not fabulous views, a Tree Walk, and a little bit of World War II history. The Upper Ride follows a paved catchwater; the Lower Ride, parallel to the Upper, is all dirt. The trail is suitable for running in many places, and a loop of Upper and Lower Lady Clementi's Ride makes a good run (about 4.4 km/2.75 m roundtrip), although parts are a bit rocky and overgrown and may need to be walked.

Distance: 5.4 km/3.5 mi	Difficulty: 2/5	Time: 2 hr 30 min
Rise: 170 m	Map 3.1	
Countryside Map Grid: • Start: 10 and 64 • Finish: 08 and 65		

3J   REPULSE BAY SEAVIEW PROMENADE Ⓓ Ⓚ Ⓡ Ⓢ

Not actually out of the Hub, but in the area and worth doing, this delightful flat stroll provides a close-up view of the South China Sea and Deep Water Bay. It can be extended to include Mills and Chung Path, which ends up by the Hong Kong Country Club. Take time to visit the fanciful temple at the south end of Repulse Bay.

Distance: 3.25 km/2 mi	Difficulty: 1/5	Time: 45 min
Rise: negligible	Map 3.3	
Countryside Map Grid: • Start: 11–12 and 61–62 • Finish: 10–11 and 62–63		

3K   CHUNG HOM KOK Ⓚ Ⓡ Ⓢ

A bit far afield from the Hub, the trail works down the spine of Chung Hom Kok. At the bottom of the peninsula, the route follows a paved road that curves along the coast and at the tip takes you to some picnic sites with marvelous views — once we saw a ray in the water here. Pirate Cheung Po Tsai's cave is supposedly here, see if you can find it. A good outing for kids, and you can run it too.

Distance: 3 km/1.9 mi	Difficulty: 1/5	Time: 45 min
Rise: 100 m	Map 3.3	
Countryside Map Grid: • Start: 11–12 and 60–61 • Finish: 11–12 and 58–59		

3L   STANLEY FORT Ⓡ Ⓢ

A long pull uphill to the old fort (now a PLA base and you are definitely not invited in) with some deep ocean views. A very good running trail, except there is quite a bit of bus traffic. Coming down, enjoy lovely views of Stanley Bay and at the bottom you can pause at the historic cemetery. There are lots of places to snack afterwards, better run it twice!

Distance: 1.5 km/0.9 mi	Difficulty: 2/5	Time: 30 min
Rise: 120 m	Map 3.3	
Countryside Map Grid: • Start: 12–13 and 59–60 • Finish: 13 and 57–58		

TAI TAM TREE WALK 🇰 🇳

A sweet little path branching off from Tai Tam Reservoir Road just inside the park, is a winner with kids.

Distance: 0.1 km/0.06 mi	Difficulty: 1/5	Time: 15 min
Rise: negligible	Map 3.2	
Countryside Map Grid: 12 and 64		

WONG NAI CHUNG TREE WALK 🇰 🇳

See Sir Cecil's Ride, Hike 3C.

Distance: 2 km/1.25 mi	Difficulty: 1/5	Time: 1 hr
Rise: negligible	Map 3.1	
Countryside Map Grid: 10–11 and 64 (not marked as a Tree Walk on the map)		

Hub Amenities

kview has a restaurant and a grocery store. The hotel has toilets and the staff is kind ut allowing people with back packs to use them. There are also public toilets at ng Nai Chung Reservoir, half-way up Tai Tam Reservoir Road from Wong Nai Chung ɔ, and on weekends a snack bar opens there. If you end up in Tai Tam, there is a et block at the park entrance; for sustenance you will have to take a cab, bus or ıibus to Stanley (5 min) or Chai Wan (20 min). There are several restaurants and a cery store in Repulse Bay.

Hike 3B finishes in Quarry Bay, which has many restaurants and shops on King's d.

Map 3.1 3A 3B 3C 3H

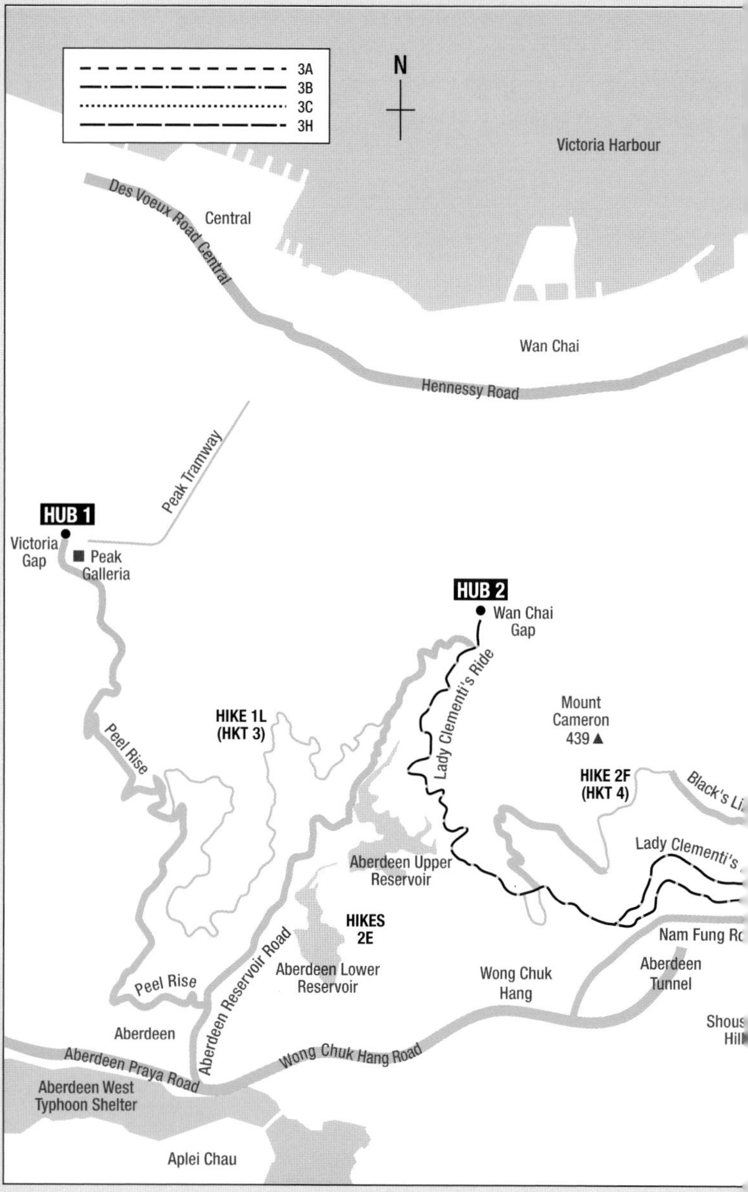

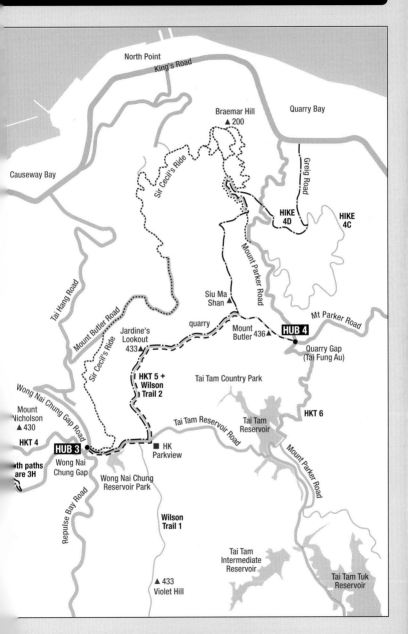

North Point

King's Road

Braemar Hill
▲ 200

Quarry Bay

Causeway Bay

Greig Road

Sir Cecil's Ride

HIKE
4D

HIKE
4C

Tai Hang Road

Mount Parker Road

Mount Butler Road

Siu Ma
Shan ▲

Mt Parker Road

quarry

Jardine's
Lookout
433▲

Mount
Butler 436 ▲

HUB 4

Quarry Gap
(Tai Fung Au)

Sir Cecil's Ride

HKT 5 +
Wilson
Trail 2

Tai Tam Country Park

Wong Nai Chung Gap Road

Mount
Nicholson
▲ 430

HKT 4

Tai Tam Reservoir Road

Tai Tam
Reservoir

HKT 6

Mount Parker Road

th paths
are 3H

HUB 3

Wong Nai
Chung Gap

■ HK
Parkview

Repulse Bay Road

Wong Nai Chung
Reservoir Park

Wilson
Trail 1

Tai Tam
Intermediate
Reservoir

Tai Tam Tuk
Reservoir

▲ 433
Violet Hill

HIKE 3C

Mount Butler Road

quarry

Jardine's
Lookout
433 ▲

HIKE 3A
(HKT 5 + Wilson Trail 2)

Tai Tam Country Park

Sir Cecil's Ride

Tai Tam Reservoir Road

Tai Tam
Reservoir

HIKE 2F
(HKT 4)

To
HIKE 3H

HUB 3

Nam Fung Road

■ HK Parkview

Wong Nai Chung
Reservoir Park

Wong Nai
Chung Gap

Repulse Bay Road

Violet Hill
▲ 433

Wilson
Trail 1

Tai Tam
Intermediate
Reservoir

Tsz Lo Lan Shan Path

Tsin Shui Wan Au

to the Twins
see Map 3.3

Hong Kong
International School ■

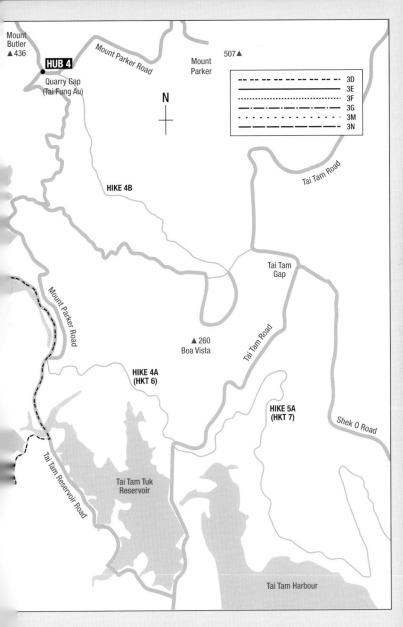

Mount
Butler
▲ 436

HUB 4

Quarry Gap
(Tai Fung Au)

Mount Parker Road

Mount
Parker

507▲

N

	3D
	3E
	3F
	3G
	3M
	3N

HIKE 4B

Tai Tam Road

Mount Parker Road

Tai Tam
Gap

▲ 260
Boa Vista

Tai Tam Road

HIKE 4A
(HKT 6)

HIKE 5A
(HKT 7)

Shek O Road

Tai Tam Reservoir Road

Tai Tam Tuk
Reservoir

Tai Tam Harbour

Map 3.3   3F   3G   2J   3K   3L

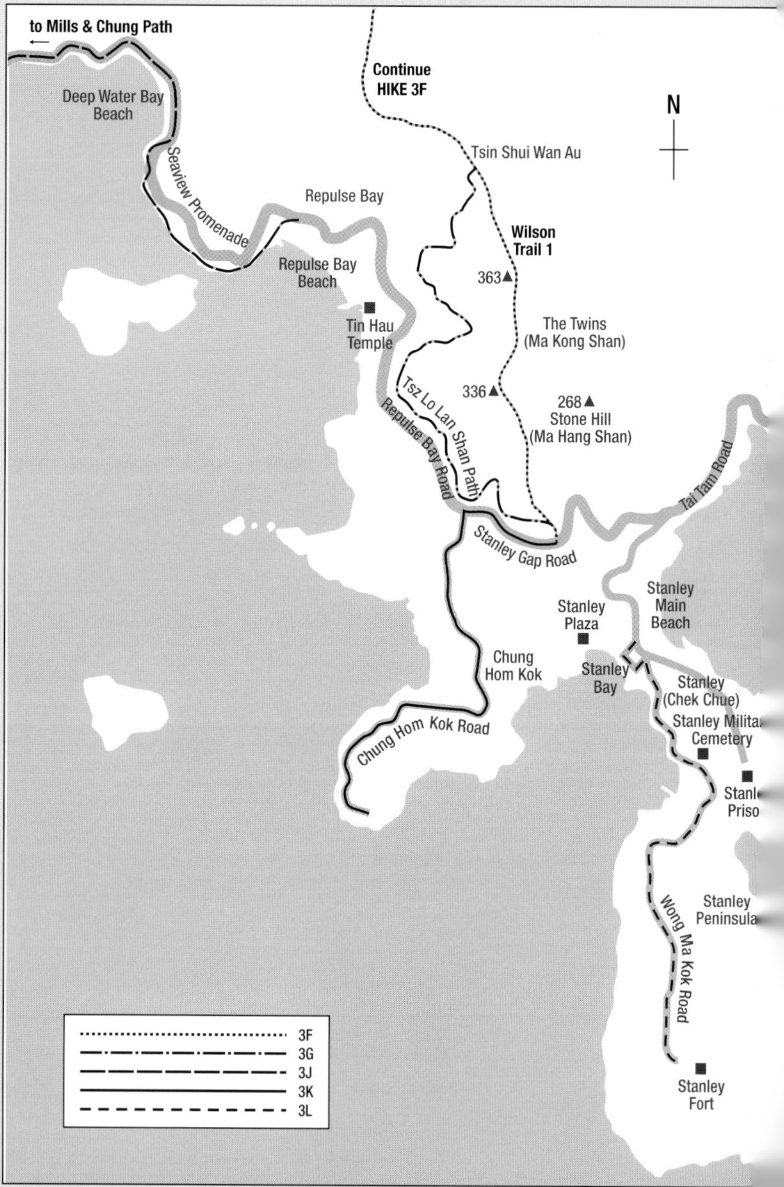

to Mills & Chung Path

Deep Water Bay
Beach

Seaview Promenade

Continue
HIKE 3F

Tsin Shui Wan Au

Repulse Bay

Wilson
Trail 1

363 ▲

Repulse Bay
Beach

Tin Hau
Temple

The Twins
(Ma Kong Shan)

336 ▲

268 ▲
Stone Hill
(Ma Hang Shan)

N

Tsz Lo Lan Shan Path

Repulse Bay Road

Tai Tam Road

Stanley Gap Road

Stanley
Plaza

Stanley
Main Beach

Chung
Hom Kok

Stanley
Bay

Stanley
(Chek Chue)

Stanley Military
Cemetery

Chung Hom Kok Road

Stanley
Prison

Stanley
Peninsula

Wong Ma Kok Road

Stanley
Fort

· · · · · · · · · · · · ·	3F
▬ ▬ ▬ ▬ ▬ ▬ ▬	3G
▬ ▬ · ▬ · ▬ · ▬	3J
▬▬▬▬▬▬▬▬	3K
▬ ▬ ▬ ▬ ▬ ▬ ▬	3L

3A HONG KONG TRAIL SECTION 5 (MOUNT BUTLER) — WONG NAI CHUNG GAP TO MOUNT PARKER ROAD

S P S

One of the most difficult yet prettiest sections of the Hong Kong Trail, Section 5 rewards your efforts with camera ready vistas. Starting just below Parkview, the trail undulates up and down, via path and stairs — lots and lots of serious stairs — over Jardine's Lookout (433 m), past the quarry and over Mount Butler (436 m) then down (stairs again) to Quarry Gap. You will need to allow time to get back to public transport — see Hub 4. Section 5 is a tough hike but well worth the effort.

> Distance: 4 km/2.5 mi
> Difficulty: 5/5
> Timing: 1 hr 30 min
> Rise: 130 m
> ⊕ Map 3.1
> Countryside Map Grid:
> Start: 11–12 and 64
> Finish: 12–13 and 65

▶ To Get There

Walk up Tai Tam Reservoir Road from Wong Nai Chung Gap Road towards Parkview. Just before Parkview there is a small car park on the left, and just east of the small car park a cluster of signs marks the beginning of the trail. There is a gateway marked with the Wilson and Hong Kong Trail signs, a marble Wilson Trail Marker and a signboard with maps. A signpost shows:

Jardine's Lookout (Hong Kong Trail Section 5 and Wilson Trail Section 2) — 4 km/2.5 mi; 1 hr 30 min — left — Hikes 3A and 3B

Quarry Gap via Siu Ma Shan (Wilson Trail) — 6.6 km/4.1 mi; 2 hr 30 min — left — Hike 3B

Violet Hill — back — Hike 3F

Wan Nai Chung Gap Road via Wong Nai Chung Reservoir — back — Hike 3E

Tai Tam Reservoir Road BBQ sites — ahead; see Hike 3D

Note: For the next few kilometers, the Wilson and Hong Kong Trails overlap. See Hike 3B.

Take the few stairs down, cross the bridge passing a BBQ site on the left, and bearing right, go up the first of many flights of stairs. You will emerge out in the open to the side of Parkview, heading north.

Pass under the electric pylon and the W009 Wilson Trail marker, continuing along the side of a chain-link fence surrounding an underground reservoir. The tall mountain beyond is Jardine's Lookout (433 m), the trail's second highest point. You can't say you weren't warned about the climb ahead! Views to the left can extend to Lamma Island, depending on the height of the shrubbery and the weather.

After marker H053, views start to broaden. Looking from south to west, you wil see Deep Water Bay, Brick Hill and Ocean Park, Aberdeen, Mount Nicholson and ever Victoria Peak. Keep climbing up Jardine's Lookout; Mount Butler (at 436 m, challeng number two) is on the right. Head up a mixture of stairs and dirt trail, around two larg boulders.

At marker H054 (Wilson Trail marker W010), the trail flattens out for a spell. A one point the shrubs are head high, but you can take a few steps off the trail and see th Tai Tam Reservoirs, and the harbor beyond. The path is quite worn here and could b slippery in damp weather. Now start up a long series of steps — at the top of the ridg you will come to a signpost and a JUNCTION:

- **Mount Butler — 1.5 km/0.9 mi; 1 hr — ahead**
- Wong Nai Chung Reservoir — 1 km/0.6 mi; 20 min — back to Tai Tam Reservo Road

Take a moment to go just beyond the trigonometric station for stupendous view to the north with all of Causeway Bay and Kowloon in sight. Back on the trail, as you g down the steep stairs, a huge quarry spreads below of you. Parkview is on your righ continue down, looking right down on the Tai Tam Reservoirs, and cross the catchwate

After passing marker H056 and a marble Wilson Trail sign, climb "the Gre Wall," ascending along the side of the quarry with many steep stairs with high rise The path is somewhat exposed and you may hear explosions booming from the quar The views of Tai Tam are glorious, and you can now look back to Parkview — but ke an eye on your feet too.

Near marker H057, after a brief but welcome respite on a short, flatter stretch mainly dirt path, pass by a boarded up tunnel/mine shaft on the left. The trail flatte out along the ridge before you reach a JUNCTION:

- **Hong Kong Trail Section 5 — Mount Butler — straight**
- Wilson Trail — left. The Wilson Trail veers off to Quarry Bay and, eventually to t New Territories, see Hike 3B.

(No distance is shown. It takes about an hour to get to this point from Parkview.)

As you walk uphill, the views encompass the entire east end of Victoria Harb with Chai Wan in the foreground and Kai Tak in the distance. Continue along the rid and up a set of serious high steps made of stone. Next, thread through some rocks a dip slightly down before beginning a second set of steps, mostly rock and dirt, pass a small cave. Conquer these steps and you are on top of Mount Butler (436 m)! Countryside Map Grid 12–13 and 65. Near marker H059, a signpost and JUNCTIO point out your alternatives:

Boa Vista — 1.25 km/0.8 mi; 30 min — ahead to Quarry Gap
Jardine's Lookout — 1.5 km/0.9 mi; 1 hr — back

There is also a view compass and a trigonometric station.

Head down very steep and uneven steps; they are very small and difficult for those big feet. It's only a short way now! There are two rest stops on the way down, and teps widen after the second stop. You soon arrive at Quarry Gap and the beginning ong Kong Trail Section 6. The signpost advises:

Quarry Bay (Mount Parker Road) — 3 km/1.9 mi; 40 min — left
Tai Tam Tuk Reservoir (Hong Kong Trail Section 6) — 4.5 km/2.8 mi; 1 hr 30 min — right; see Hike 4A
Wong Nai Chung via Mount Butler (Hong Kong Trail Section 5) — 4 km/2.5 mi; 1 hr 30 min — back

To Continue to Hike

See above signpost

Mount Parker Road to Boa Vista Hill — straight ahead, look for a small sign for Boa Vista Hill on the right side of the road; see Hike 4B

Mount Parker Road to the Quarry Bay Tree Walk or Hong Pak Country Trail; see Hikes 4C, 4D

Sir Cecil's Ride — Hike 3C

To Leave the Trail

Quarry Bay — 3 km/1.9 mi; 20 min — via Mount Parker Road — left
South down Mount Parker Road to return to Tai Tam via Tai Tam Reservoir Road — about 45 min — right

Quarry Gap has toilets, a telephone, a small fitness area and several BBQ sites. e is also a map board.

3B WILSON TRAIL SECTION 2 — PARKVIEW TO QUARRY BAY

Challenging, with lots of hills and stairs, this trail climbs Jardine's Lookout (433 m), aptly named for its far-reaching views to the north. The trail then dips down to pass the quarry, which is not its most scenic point. As compensation, after you pass the quarry the views are unmatched. Unlike the Hong Kong Trail Section 5 (Hike 3A) this trail does not climb Mount Butler, but it does crest Siu Ma Shan, which despite the "siu" (small) in its name is almost as tall as Mount Butler, about 420 m. You finish in Quarry Bay.

> Distance: 6.6 km/4.1 mi
> Difficulty: 5/5
> Time: 2 hr 30 min
> Rise: 230 m
> Map 3.1
> Countryside Map Grid:
> Start: 11–12 and 64
> Finish: 13 and 67

 ### To Get There

Walk up Tai Tam Reservoir Road from Wong Nai Chung Gap Road towards Parkv Just before Parkview there is a small car park on the left, and just east of the smal park, a cluster of signs marks the beginning of the trail. There is a gateway marked the Wilson and Hong Kong Trail signs, a marble Wilson Trail Marker and a signb with maps. A signpost shows:

- **Quarry Gap via Siu Ma Shan (Wilson Trail Section 2) — 6.6 km/4.1 mi; 2 hr 30 — left**
- Jardine's Lookout (Hong Kong Trail Section 5 and Wilson Trail Section 2) — 4 2.5 mi; 1 hr 30 min — left — Hike 3A
- Violet Hill — back — Hike 3F
- Wan Nai Chung Gap Road via Wong Nai Chung Reservoir — back — Hike 3
- Tai Tam Reservoir Road BBQ sites — ahead; see Hike 3D

Note: For the next few kilometers, the Wilson and Hong Kong Trails overlap. See Hike

Take the few stairs down, cross the bridge passing a BBQ site on the left, bearing right, go up the first of many flights of stairs. You will emerge out in the ope the side of Parkview, heading north.

Pass under the electric pylon and the W009 Wilson Trail marker, continuing a the side of a chain-link fence surrounding an underground reservoir. The tall moun beyond is Jardine's Lookout (433 m), the trail's highest point. You can't say you we warned about the climb ahead! Views to the left can extend to Lamma Island, depen on the height of the shrubbery and the weather.

After marker H053, views start to broaden. You pass a wooden marker for the
g Kong Trail and the Country Trail, Hike 3E. Looking from south to west, you will
Deep Water Bay, Brick Hill and Ocean Park, Aberdeen, Mount Nicholson and even
oria Peak. Keep climbing up Jardine's Lookout; Mount Butler is on the right. Head
mixture of stairs and dirt trail, around two large boulders.

At marker H054 (Wilson Trail marker W010), the trail flattens out for a spell. At
point the shrubs are head high, but you can take a few steps off the trail and see the
Tam Reservoirs, and the harbor beyond. The path is quite worn here and could be
very in damp weather. Now start up a long series of steps; at the top of the ridge you
come to a signpost and a JUNCTION:

Mount Butler — 1.5 km/0.9 mi; 1 hr — ahead

Wong Nai Chung Reservoir — 1 km/0.6 mi; 20 min — back to Tai Tam Reservoir
Road

Take a moment to go just beyond the trigonometric station for stupendous views
e north with all of Causeway Bay and Kowloon in sight. Back on the trail, as you go
n the steep stairs, a huge quarry spreads in front of you. Parkview is on your right;
w the trail down, looking right down on the Tai Tam Reservoirs, and cross the
hwater.

After passing marker H056 and a marble Wilson Trail sign, climb "the Great
l," ascending along the side of the quarry with many steep stairs with high risers.
path is somewhat exposed and you may hear explosions booming from the quarry.
views of Tai Tam are glorious, and you can now look back to Parkview — but keep
ye on your feet too.

Near marker H057, after a brief welcome respite on a short and flatter stretch of
nly dirt path, you will pass by a boarded up tunnel/mine shaft on the left. The trail
ens out along the ridge before you reach a JUNCTION:

Wilson Trail — left

Hong Kong Trail Section 5 — Mount Butler — straight

distance is shown. It takes about an hour to get to this point form Parkview.)

Follow the Wilson Trail left (north) up the paved rock steps to the top of Siu Ma
ı (420 m); the trail then becomes dirt. You will suddenly come upon views stretching
Lei Yue Mun, the narrowest part of the shipping channel, to Kai Tak, the former
ort. Follow the trail up and over, down and up to pass marker W013, where a dirt
detours left out to a point for another vista. Stay on the main path past the unsightly
trical tower on the right hand side; then begin going down. A sweeping 180-degree
y takes in the west end of the Island to the east beyond Lei Yue Mun — a greater
orama is hard to find.

You can see the trail rolling in front of you, through low shrubs and grass; r[...]
paved stairs change to a rocky dirt path up and over a hill. A short way back down [...]
the dirt trail travels down to very seriously steep stairs. The good news is that th[...]
stairs are all rock-paved and are wide enough to make each step comfortable.

Cross over Siu Ma Shan Bridge, marked with a very special marble and gold s[...]
The Wilson Trail veers right at the Wilson post marker and follows a dirt path. O[...]
dirt trails fanning out in all directions lead to Hong Kong Telecom masts, which are [...]
limits.

At marker W015, a sign identifies the Mount Butler H.F. Radio Receiving Sta[...]
also off-limits. Very soon the trail becomes a rock-paved path stepping down about [...]
steps beside a lovely stream on the right; you can now see Kornhill in front of you. [...]
may be pre-occupied, however, with another set of stairs descending steeply to a [...]
Turn left, with a sigh of relief, to a JUNCTION:

- **The Wilson Trail — left (marble marker)**
- Quarry Bay Jogging Trail — left or right — you are 500 meters from the Brae[...]
  Hill end of the jogging trail
- Sir Cecil's Ride — left (also overlaps jogging trail); see Hike 3C

Shortly, another sign points to Sir Cecil's Ride to the left. **Stay to the right on[...]
flat jogging trail** to marker W016, a JUNCTION:

- **Mount Parker Road — right**
- Tai Fung Au (Quarry Gap) — left

Enough of the flat trail, it's now back to serious business down ever more s[...]
(about 250), but this brief section has some real treats as you drop into the trees[...]
pass a charming and well-tended set of shrines and sitting-out areas. At a rocky out[...]
the statue of Kwan Yin serenely blesses passers-by. **Follow the Wilson Trail sign[...]
the right**, down past more flat open areas and some exercise bars. Pass to the far e[...]
a shelter and down the final set of stairs, reaching a covered pavilion and signboa[...]
Mount Parker Road.

CHOICES:
- Quit now, by walking down Mount Parker Road to King's Road. The Conserv[...]
  Association has posted some signs with environmental information along the [...]
- Complete the last leg of the "official" trail — left and down Mount Parker [...]
  about 250 meters to the next Wilson Trail marker and the very well-marked Qu[...]
  Bay Tree Walk, Hike 4D.

If you elect to continue, proceed down the stairs, and then up and past an old ruin. It is not identified but it might have been a wartime storeroom. At marker W017, look for the outdoor wok stoves built as public kitchens in 1938–39. These were intended to feed people displaced from their homes by the impending Japanese invasion. Since the battles lasted only a few days, the kitchens were never used.

Follow the path as it heads up to stairs and to another public kitchen. A sign shows Morning Walkers' Garden on the right. The Tree Walk continues to the left through the north side of this second kitchen, down a series of stairs, past a picnic table, and across a bridge over a stream. Soon you reach the Kornhill BBQ site and a sign:

- **Kornhill — forward**
- Tai Fung Au (Quarry Gap) — back

Pass the flat paved area that holds a shelter and more remnants of the public kitchens, as well as some play equipment. Then go down stairs past another BBQ site to a JUNCTION:

- **Wilson Trail to Quarry Bay — left**
  Mount Parker Road (Hong Pak Country Trail — 3.6 km/2.25 mi; 1 hr 45 min — Hike 4C) — ahead (this sign is odd, as the quickest way to Mount Parker Road is back)
  Wilson Trail to Wong Nai Chung Reservoir via Quarry Gap/Tai Fung Au — back — Hikes 3B, 3C

There is a map board of the Hong Pak Country Trail — Hike 4C.

Follow the catchwater, which must have been a charming stream before it was covered with concrete and stripped of all natural beauty, to a paved area with a bench, map board showing the Wilson Trail, a sign for the Quarry Bay Country Park, and a marble marker that says "The Wilson Trail Tai Koo Section."

Cross the paved area and turn left down the stairs and along a concrete path in front of a very large apartment complex. Pass W018 as you reach the exit at Greig Road. Follow Greig Road downhill to King's Road and turn right to reach the MTR (Tai Koo Station).

To Continue to Hike

Return to Sir Cecil's Ride for more hiking; see Hike 3C

Hong Pak Country Trail — back up Mount Parker Road to the Country Trail — Hike 4C

3C *SIR CECIL'S RIDE*

𝐊 𝐍 𝐑 𝐒

This is an excellent hike with a lot of variety. The trail first offers very good views of Victoria Harbor from a fairly level path, which is also a Tree Walk. After a brief stint uphill on a paved road, the trail becomes a flat path just above Causeway Bay and takes you to Braemar Hill (200 m); be sure to detour to the top of the hill for a terrific view. Finally, the path connects with the flat Quarry Bay Jogging Trail and ends at Mount Parker Road in Quarry Bay. It can be run in many parts. The Braemar Hill section and the Tree Walk (at the beginning) are good for kids too. Sir Cecil's Ride is one of our longer hikes but there are lots of places to leave the trail if you decide you've had enough for the day.

> Distance: 8.9 km/5.6 mi
> Difficulty: 2/5
> Time: 3 hr
> Rise: negligible
> Map 3.1
> Countryside Map Grid:
> • Start: 10–11 and 64
> • Finish: 12–13 and 66

To Get There

Take the stairs just uphill from the gas station on Wong Nai Chung Gap Road and ma[...] an immediate left turn. If you are coming down Tai Tam Reservoir Road, either take [...] path to the right between the bridge and the little park or the steps just beyond the [...] park driveway. At our last visit, the signboard at the top of these steps had a sha[...] warning poster — you just aren't safe anywhere in Hong Kong! At the bottom of [...] stairs, you will see a map board, and a Tree Walk marker.

Follow the lovely, flat, tree-lined dirt walk past several plant identification mark[...] as it winds around apartment buildings.

Pass marker C4109, in back of the Cricket Club, soon arriving at a picnic [...] overlooking the club grounds and Mount Nicholson (430 m) beyond. **An emerge[...] phone is nearby**.

After passing another picnic area and a concrete shelter that has tables and benc[...] follow a rock-paved path to a JUNCTION:

- **Sir Cecil's Ride — ahead**
- Tai Hang Road (Happy Valley) — steps down to the left
- Parkview — right, up steep steps. Cross over a covered reservoir, then up m[...] stairs to a catchwater; turn right to Tai Tam Reservoir Road.

Shortly, you arrive at a second JUNCTION and a signpost:

Mount Butler Road — 0.8 km/0.5 mi; 15 min — ahead
Parkview (Tai Tam Country Trail) — steps to the right; see Hike 3E
Tai Hang Road (Happy Valley) — stairs down to the left
Tai Tam Reservoir Road — 1.6 km/1 mi; 30 min — back

As you travel on, pass more sets of stairs going down to Tai Hang Road. Shortly, reach a stone marker indicating "Home Affairs Dept. Project" on the right. There is d urn here and Chinese characters inscribed in the wall; red poles form an entrance leads up to well-tended gardens. If you reach this point in the morning, you will bably find elderly people playing mahjong and practicing Tai Chi. **There is a phone next to the gate**.

Back along the main path, follow concrete steps with dirt on either side across he streambeds. The path turns right as you head up stairs. You soon reach a CTION:

Sir Cecil's Ride — left
Explore a lovely group of well-kept shrines — straight and up stairs

Crossing more streams, finish the Tree Walk section by taking stairs down to the to Mount Butler Road and your CHOICES:

Sir Cecil's Ride — right
Go home — Just after a signpost that says "Wong Nai Chung Tree Walk — 2 km," a set of stairs to the left leads to the intersection of Mount Butler Road and Henderson Road, and a bus stop for minibus No. 24 to Admiralty, or bus No. 11 to Central Piers/Admiralty. See Countryside Map Grid: 10–11 and 65.

The path runs parallel to Mount Butler Road briefly, before descending to the road a sign indicating "Sir Cecil's Ride." At this point, Sir Cecil's Ride overlaps the heavily icked road, but only for a short distance. There are no sidewalks; stay to the right e of the road for safest navigation, as you proceed up the hill to a JUNCTION/rsection:

Mount Butler Range — right towards the Quarry
Mount Butler Road No. 111 — left

As the road slopes down, you pass buildings first on your right, then on your left. might come across some stray dogs in this area, but when we passed by they were aggressive. Climb a gradual rise to a JUNCTION:

A narrow road — straight ahead. A sign reads Mount Butler Receiving Station and Sir Cecil's Ride (hidden behind the "Do Not Enter" sign for the range)

- Mount Butler Range — right uphill behind a gate. Not open to the public.
Note: The road downhill to the left leads to an industrial area.

As you follow the straight road uphill, enjoy the expansive views of the harbor city, from Causeway Bay all the way to Victoria Peak. Looking back you will get a view of the quarry.

As you approach the end of the road, before the entrance to the Hong Kong Tele Receiving Station (off limits — and they mean it) take **a little concrete path to the into the bamboo thicket, lying between two large traffic mirrors and marked w blue and red painted arrows on the pavement.**

The concrete disappears quickly, leaving a washed out, but passable dirt trail, wh travels along an exposed ledge with another good view of Causeway Bay. There little **trail out to the edge of the cliff for a better view**. The main path altern between dirt and concrete; there are nice views across the Island from Victoria Pea the harbor. Suddenly the path broadens out overlooking St. Joan of Arc School College as well as Choi Sai Woo Park, in North Point.

At the time of this writing, this section of the trail was fairly overgrown, but passable. If you feel unprotected, look for the two gods sitting in a small shrine on side of the trail. You have some CHOICES:

- **Mount Parker Road — straight**
- To leave the trail — left down the hill on the pavement to find minibus No. 2 Admiralty from St. Joan of Arc School, North Point. See Countryside Map (11–12 and 67–68.

The concrete path, which turns into dirt, affords views of Braemar Hill. Ignore stairs that head steeply up the hill to the right, signed Braemar Hill Fresh Water Ser Reservoir. Pass behind a large apartment complex on a good dirt path, then cross (a stream to reach a delightful area with a full flowing stream, a shelter, and a woo signpost that indicates "Tai Tam County Park, Quarry Bay Extension." This is a peac spot for a rest.

There is a maze of trails in this area, all of which end up at Mount Parker Road. will see Sir Cecil's name on many paths, making it difficult to identify an exact path. describe one enjoyable route; explore the many others at your leisure!

Pass through the wooden posts (placed there to block bike riding) and enjoy flat dirt path that heads toward the 2,500-meter (2.5 km/1.6 mi) Quarry Bay Jogg Trail. To the left is Po Luen Path, which becomes Po Luen Road and links to Tin I Temple Road in Braemar Hill. See Countryside Map Grid 12 and 67–68. Soon you a JUNCTION:

- **Stay on the path — ahead**
- A short distance ahead, stairs to the right lead to Mount Parker Road. They take you up to a small gap (continue straight at the junction), then along more steps down to the Quarry Bay Jogging Trail/Wilson Trail/Sir Cecil's Ride — a bit of a shortcut.

Now another JUNCTION, affording you two routes to the top of Braemar Hill 200 m):

- Ahead up and down a brief set of stairs to the 500-meter marker of the jogging trail and Mount Parker Road; at the top of the stairs is a sign pointing left for Braemar Hill.
- Left to reach the beginning of the jogging trail (going around Braemar Hill). (This section can also be reached via Braemar Hill Road, which circles north of Choi Sai Woo Park.) At the beginning of the jogging trail, stairs heading steeply uphill to the right also lead you in short order to the top of Braemar Hill.

Return to the flat and mostly dirt jogging trail, which winds in and out of the trees s it heads south to connect with Mount Parker Road. Along the way you will see the arrow harbor passage at Lei Yue Mun. The trail is marked with a yellow jogging figure, d is very easy to follow.

After the 1,000/1,500-meter post, there is a JUNCTION:

Wilson Trail to Kornhill (at marker W016) — right — overlapping the Quarry Bay Jogging Trail

Mount Parker Road — stairs down ahead. You pass a lovely temple and two routes to Mount Parker Road

Tai Fung Au (Quarry Gap) — back along the jogging trail

And then yet another JUNCTION:

Wilson Trail/Quarry Bay Jogging Trail — left

Sir Cecil's Ride — right

Mount Parker Road — left

Pass the 1,500/1,000-meter marker of the jogging trail, and just before the 2,000/)-meter marker, reach a JUNCTION:

Jogging trail to Mount Parker Road — unmarked — ahead

Wilson Trail — right — up steep stairs

At Mount Parker Road, there is a map board with an Orienteering Course and a 1 for Sir Cecil's Ride.

To Continue to Hike

- As you go down Mount Parker Road, pick up the Wilson Trail as it crosses to the east; this last section is well marked as the Quarry Bay Tree Walk. Only 1.1 km/0.7 mi to Kornhill, it passes World War II ruins and is a worthwhile detour; see Hike 3B and 4D.

- Hong Pak Country Trail — go up Mount Parker Road and turn left at the Quarry Bay Management Centre, Tai Tam Country Park — Hike 4C

 ## To Leave the Trail

- Descend Mount Parker Road, which is quite steep, past lovely BBQ areas, and Woodside House. When you reach King's Road, turn right to the Tai Koo MTR station.

D TAI TAM RESERVOIR COUNTRY PARK LOOP

Ⓓ Ⓚ Ⓝ Ⓡ Ⓢ

Tam Country Park is a huge preserve in the middle
e south side of the Island and contains three beautiful
rvoirs. The loop circles the Intermediate Reservoir.
Tam Reservoir Road traverses the park steeply
nhill from Parkview to Tai Tam Road, with views of
reservoirs and Shek O Peninsula that are simply
itiful. The rest of the loop is less scenic but a pretty
to go "off road" and a good link to other hikes. The
can be very busy on weekends, full of people making
d use of the many picnic and BBQ sites. The road and
er Reservoir Path are good for running.

> Distance: 6 km/3.8 mi
> Difficulty: 2/5
> Time: 2 hr
> Rise: 300 m
> Ⓝ Map 3.2
> Countryside Map Grid:
> - Start and Finish:
>   11–12 and 64.
> - Repulse Bay Gap is just
>   northwest of 12 and 62.
> - Tai Tam Reservoir Road
>   meets Tai Tam Road at
>   13–14 and 62.

To Get There

m Wong Nai Chung Gap walk up Tai Tam Reservoir Road to Parkview. Beyond the
ance to Parkview, as the road turns downhill, there is a gate and sign for Tai Tam
ntry Park.

At marker T8201, the paved road runs down the hill, past a picnic site on the left
a BBQ site on the right, a clue to the popularity of this site on weekends and
days. Toilet facilities can be found on the left as well as a second BBQ site. Further
n the road, across from the Tai Tam Country Park Tai Tam Management Centre
ding, is the signed Tai Tam Tree Walk (Hike 3M) as well as BBQ site No. 3. Follow
g the road, uphill now, reaching BBQ site No. 4 on the left and then a gate, a shelter
signboard for the Tai Tam Country Park on your right.

The road narrows and you quickly reach marker T8202 and head seriously down
hill; you can see Shek O Road in the distance winding along underneath Dragon's
k, Hike 5B. Tree markers border the road. Crossing the stream, the road winds down
under the trees until it reaches the bottom side of the Upper Tai Tam Reservoir.
t miss the waterfall on the left as the road curves right and reaches a dam:

**Turn right before the dam at a sign reading "Wong Nai Chung Gap Road
2 km/1.25 mi; 45 min" and walk along a smaller bridge over a finger of
the reservoir.**

103

Pick up the path to Repulse Bay Gap along the concrete catchwater Governm⬛ warning signs remind you to use the trail at your own risk, but it is not really ⬛ dangerous. Four or five times you will cross a streambed on a narrow concrete be⬛ but for most of the trail you will follow a fairly wide track suitable for running. The ⬛ is wooded and shady with occasional glimpses of the reservoirs glinting in the sun⬛

After 10 minutes or so you will see a concrete path downhill to the right. This conn⬛ with the Lower Reservoir Path (described below), an option if you do not want to go al⬛ way to Repulse Bay Gap.

At the end, the trail leaves the catchwater and becomes a dirt path for a short ⬛ before joining the Wilson Trail. The path takes about 45 minutes, at a walking p⬛ You will come upon the Wilson Trail just 250 steps above the gap. You have s⬛ CHOICES:

- **Tai Tam Tuk — the Lower Reservoir Path to Tai Tam Reservoir Roa⬛ 1.3 km/0.8 mi; 40 min — turn left downhill to the map signboard at Rep⬛ Bay Gap. Cross the bridge and turn left along the Lower Reservoir P⬛ marked "to Tai Tam Tuk".**
- Violet Hill — 1.1 km/0.7 mi; 45 min — right — Hike 3F
- Wong Nai Chung Reservoir — 2.7 km/1.7 mi; 1 hr 30 min — ahead — Hike
- Wilson Trail — left, downhill and across the bridge to stairs up to the right, ta⬛ you to the Twins and on to Stanley; see Hike 3F.
- Repulse Bay — left and down the steps. Before the bridge, take the unmarked ⬛ to the right, and to the right of the Stanley West Catchwater sign. The trail ca⬛ overgrown. It disgorges you at the Hong Kong International School Elemen⬛ School campus in South Bay, after traversing jumbled rocks in a streambed.
- Stanley — left and down the steps. Follow the catchwater to the right, before ⬛ bridge — Hike 3G.

At the beginning section of the Lower Reservoir Path, after a flat start, the ⬛ climbs down steadily, as you scramble over rocks and narrow concrete bridges ⬛ streams. Then the trail alternates between flat sections and rocky areas, as well as betw⬛ gentle ups and downs. Streambeds flowing toward the reservoir can be quite rocky; ⬛ section of the path is deeply rutted and a bit difficult to negotiate.

The path returns you to Tai Tam Reservoir Road about 1.2 km/0.75 mi from ⬛ Tam Road.

To Continue to Hike

- Back up Tai Tam Reservoir Road to the start — left
- Mount Parker Road to Boa Vista Hill — left — Hike 4B
- Hong Kong Trail Section 5 (Mount Butler) — left — Hike 3A
- Hong Kong Trail Section 6 — left — Hike 4A
- Hong Kong Trail Section 7 — Tai Tam Road to To Tei Wan — either turn left on Tai Tam Reservoir Road to Hong Kong Trail 6, Hike 4A, or turn right on Tai Tam Reservoir Road to Tai Tam Road, then cross Tai Tam Road to continue down the hill on Tai Tam Reservoir Road, bear left at the fork (do not go to the Hong Kong International School), then turn left to follow the waterfront, meandering through some abandoned village homes and along the bottom of the dam. On the far side of the dam, a path leads uphill, joining Section 7 at its start; see Hike 5A.

To Leave the Trail

- Right — down along the road, passing several more BBQ areas along the way. Pass markers T8207 and T8208. Crossing several bridges as the road curves alongside Tai Tam Tuk Reservoir, the trail finally meets Tai Tam Road. Note that walking on Tai Tam Road is not recommended. Buses, minibuses and taxis are available.

Alternatives

Find the Lower Reservoir Path to Repulse Bay Gap on Tai Tam Reservoir Road: About 1.2 km/0.75 mi from Tai Tam Road, near BBQ Site No. 3, at the Tai Tam end of a bridge, there is a sign for Tai Tam Intermediate Reservoir (on the right as you walk towards Tai Tam Road.)

ote: Signs warn: "Danger, Keep Out, Floods Violently Without Warning." Many people hike this trail safely, but avoid it in or after wet weather.

If you simply want to walk down Tai Tam Reservoir Road, cross over the dam at the Upper Reservoir to a JUNCTION:

- **Tai Tam Road — 1.75 km/1 mi; 45 min — right**
- Mount Butler (Hong Kong Trail Section 6) — 2 km/1.25 mi; 1 hr — left; see Hike 4A
- Tai Tam Country Park Management Center — 0.75 km/0.5 mi; 15 min — back

The trail overlaps Hong Kong Trail Section 6 (Hike 4A) as you travel south. Keep going down the hill passing picnic and BBQ sites. On the left you will find a 3-sided concrete obelisk, probably a former boundary marker. (They are also found on the Morning Walk [Hike 1B] and on Bowen Road [Hike 2B].) Pass Marker T8204 and BBQ sites No. 6 and No. 7 as you walk steadily down hill to a flat area and BBQ site No. 4. Passing marker T8206, you will reach two JUNCTIONS:

- Mount Parker Road — left up the steep road. From here you can hike:

    Mount Butler and Boa Vista Hill — Hike 4B

    Hong Kong Trail Section 5 to Wong Nai Chung Gap — Hike 3A

- Tai Tam Reservoir — 0.75 km/0.6 mi; 30 min — back

and

- **Tai Tam Tuk Reservoir (Tai Tam Road) — 1.75 km/1.0 mi; 30 min — ahead**
- Hong Kong Trail Section 7 — 1 km/0.6 mi; 30 min — left up the stairs — Hike 5A

3E TAI TAM COUNTRY TRAIL

This versatile hike combines four different trails. First, ir Cecil's Ride, flat and easy; next, a steep climb to a path long a catchwater. After crossing back over Tai Tam eservoir Road, the route over the Wilson Trail combines at and easy sections with big climbs, and you can detour the top of Violet Hill (433 m), where the view is nmatched. For the last leg, return to Wong Nai Chung eservoir. Wonderful views without a killer workout make is hike a winner.

> Distance: 5.2 km/3.3 mi
> Difficulty: 4/5
> Time: 2 hr 30 min
> Rise: 100 m
> Map 3.2
> Countryside Map Grid:
> Start and Finish: 11–12 and 64
> The loop extends from 10–11 and 64–65 to 11–12 and 63.

To Get There

ke the stairs just uphill from the gas station on Wong Nai Chung Gap Road and make immediate left turn. If you are coming down Tai Tam Reservoir Road, either take the th to the right between the bridge and the little park or the steps just beyond the car rk driveway. At our last visit, the signboard at the top of these steps had a shark rning poster — you just aren't safe anywhere in Hong Kong!

At the bottom of the stairs, you see a map board, and a Tree Walk marker. The trail also marked with C markers at intervals. Follow the lovely, flat, tree-lined dirt walk st several plant identification markers as it winds around some apartment buildings.

Pass marker C4109 in back of the Cricket Club, soon arriving at a picnic site erlooking the club grounds and Mount Nicholson (430 m) beyond. An **emergency one is nearby**. After passing another picnic area and a concrete shelter that has les and benches, follow a rock-paved path before reaching a JUNCTION:

Country Trail — ahead
Tai Hang Road (Happy Valley) — steps down to the left
Parkview — right, up steep steps. Cross over a covered reservoir, then up more stairs to a catchwater; turn right to Tai Tam Reservoir Road.

Shortly, a second JUNCTION and a signpost:

Parkview (Tai Tam Country Trail) — steps to the right
Tai Hang Road (Happy Valley) — stairs down to the left
Mount Butler Road (Sir Cecil's Ride) — 0.8 km/0.5 mi; 15 min — ahead — Hike 3C
Tai Tam Reservoir Road — 1.6 km/1 mi; 30 min — back

Climb the many steps until you reach a concrete wall and come out on the north side of the covered reservoir. A sign identifies Jardine's Lookout Number 2 Fresh Water Service Reservoir; there are delightful views to the north. Cross over the top of the reservoir to the south and up more stairs next to a similar sign. A country trail marker of a hiking figure with a stick shows you the way.

Keep climbing, up many stairs, and pass a shelter where you can take a break before continuing up more stairs to marker C4107 and a catchwater. The trail is not clearly marked at this point.

- **Country Trail — right**
- Hong Kong Trail Section 5 — left, to the east around the hill above the quarry along the catchwater — Hike 3A.
- Tai Tam Reservoir Road — up a bit of trail and then up through the bushes to Tai Tam Reservoir Road. The trail became overgrown long ago so bring your machete.

Follow the catchwater past a country trail hiking figure marker. Views of the Tai Tam Reservoir and Ocean Park open up in front of you as you walk back towards Tai Tam Reservoir Road. You soon take a short set of stairs up to a landing, then go down a paved road, passing under electrical lines, to a gate, just west of the very small parking area on Tai Tam Reservoir Road. To your left, signposts lay out your CHOICES:

- **Violet Hill — downhill (no distance noted but it is 1.1 km/0.7 mi; 30 min)**
- Jardine's Lookout (Wilson Trail Section 2 and Hong Kong Trail Section 5) — 4 km/ 2.5 mi; 1 hr 30 min — left
- Quarry Gap via Siu Ma San (Wilson Trail Section 2) — 6.6 km/4.1 mi; 2 hr 30 min — left
- Tai Tam Reservoir Road BBQ sites — ahead
- Wong Nai Chung Gap Road via Wong Nai Chung Reservoir — downhill

Cross over Tai Tam Reservoir Road and turn right (west) going down hill a short distance to a signboard marking both the Tai Tam Country Trail and the Wilson Trail Stanley Section (Section 1, see Hike 3F). The two trails overlap for a time and are marked with both C (Country Trail) and W (Wilson Trail) distance posts.

March directly up the very steep set of stairs that seem to slant just the wrong way at the fence, follow the pebble and concrete block path as it heads right, alongside Parkview. It levels off here, only to go up a few stairs to marker C4105. Continue along the fence, then up a series of stairs to another flat, dirt section with very high bushes on both sides. Small lookouts offer impressive views both to the north (Tai Tam Country Park) and to the south (Aberdeen and Lamma Island).

The path follows stairs gently down and you pass marker W008 along a flat ection. Look back for good views to Parkview before treading up a series of many tairs. At the top of the stairs it is flat again before gently stepping down.

Suddenly the trail comes out into the open: there are welcome views of Chai Wan, Lower Tai Tam Reservoir and Tai Tam Harbor; then press on, to a JUNCTION:

- **Repulse Bay Gap/The Twins — 1.5 km/0.9 mi; 45 min — ahead — follow a dirt path further up to the top of the hill and the trigonometric station; a 360-degree view rewards your efforts. You are on top of Violet Hill (433 m); see Hike 3F.**
- Wong Nai Chung Reservoir — 1.5 km/0.9 mi; 30 min— right
- Hong Kong Parkview — 1 km/0.6 mi; 30 min — back

Two marble markers display the Wilson Trail symbol.

Return down to the junction and take the trail marked "Wong Nai Chung Reservoir." You will see Tai Tam Reservoir Road just to the left of Parkview in the distance. Take concrete stairs down to dirt stairs under the trees, then proceed along flat section with the brush high on both sides. After marker C4103, and another ries of steep dirt stairs, the trail begins to slope down; then you can see the route up front of you as you work your way down a difficult rocky and rutted path. The path ntinues to alternate between short flat areas and steep to very steep rocky or dirt ctions, peaking at another trigonometric station and a spectacular 360-degree view. rning towards Parkview, with Central in the background, the trail descends down st marker C4102.

Finally, concrete steps lead down to a shelter; then even more concrete stairs zigzag wn to a catchwater and marker C4101 as well as a sign for Violet Hill (1.1 km/0.7 mi; min). Walk left for a short distance along the catchwater to a JUNCTION:

Wong Nai Chung Reservoir — right

Repulse Bay Gap — ahead, along the catchwater (Tsz Lo Lan Shan Path) (no time noted but it is about 45 min to the gap) — Hike 3G

Violet Hill — back — 1 km/0.6 mi; 30 min

As you proceed right, you will soon reach another JUNCTION, but both routes e you to Tai Tam Reservoir Road:

Right up a steep set of stairs, then across the dam, to exit at Tai Tam Reservoir Road just west (downhill) from the Wong Nai Chung Reservoir Park.

Straight, alongside the driveway to No. 3 Repulse Bay Road Apartments and No. 5 Celestial Garden, to Tai Tam Reservoir Road.

Note: Just down the hill is the Wong Nai Chung Reservoir Park Fitness Trail. It is a pocket park located down a few stairs, beside a lovely stream, with a tiny fitness course tucked into it.

 *Alternatives*

If you start from the Hub as we just did, you actually start in the middle of the hike. The official start is at the Wong Nai Chung Reservoir Park, where a covered signboard show the Tai Tam Country Park Trail. The park is halfway up Tai Ram Reservoir Road t Parkview.

F

S P X

WILSON TRAIL SECTION 1 — VIOLET HILL *AND* THE TWINS

iolet Hill is a short intense climb up from Parkview
ng the Wilson Trail, to a spectacular 360-degree view.
er you have had your fill of the landscape, continue
r Repulse Bay Gap to the Twins, one of the most
llenging trails on Hong Kong Island. We tried to count
steps (rumored to be 1,200) but ran out of breath.
 views are among the best available, and a just reward
 all your puffing and panting. Not up for the Twins?
r options at Repulse Bay Gap range from a quick return,
 long circle around the Tai Tam Reservoirs, or a lope
r to Stanley; see Hikes 3D, 3E and 3G.

Distance: 4.8 km/3 mi
Difficulty: 5/5
Time: 2 hr
Rise: 386 m
N Map 3.2 and 3.3
Countryside Map Grid:
• Start: 11–12 and 64
• Finish: 12–13 and 60–61

To Get There

lk up Tai Tam Reservoir Road to just west/downhill of Parkview. On the right (south)
 of the road, a covered signboard marks the Tai Tam Country Trail (Hike 3E) and a
rble block identifies the Stanley Section of the Wilson Trail, Section 1. The two trails
rlap for a time and are marked with both C (Country Trail) and W (Wilson Trail)
ance posts.

Head directly up the very steep set of stairs that seem to slant just the wrong way;
he fence, follow the pebble and concrete block path as it heads right, alongside
kview. It levels off here, only to go up a few stairs to marker C4105. Continue along
 fence, then up a series of stairs to another flat, dirt section with very high bushes on
h sides. Small lookouts offer impressive views both to the north (Tai Tam Country
k) and to the south (Aberdeen and Lamma Island).

The path follows stairs gently down and you pass marker W008 along a flat dirt
tion. Look back for good views to Parkview before treading up a series of many
rs. At the top of the stairs it is flat again before gently stepping down.

Passing marker C4104 the trail begins a series of rocky flat sections interspersed
h steep dirt stairs. Suddenly the trail comes out into the open with great views of
ai Wan, Lower Tai Tam Reservoir and Tai Tam Harbor; press on, up to another flat
tion and proceed to the JUNCTION:

- **Repulse Bay Gap/the Twins— 1.5 km/0.9 mi; 45 min — ahead**
- Wong Nai Chung Reservoir — 1.3 km/0.8 mi; 30 min — right
- Hong Kong Parkview — 1.1 km/0.7 mi; 30 min — back

A marble marker displays the Wilson trail symbol.

Climb the rocky dirt trail uphill to a trigonometric station on the top of Violet ▮ (433 m) and a spectacular view.

Now begins a long descent, at times fairly flat along a ridge, at times up a sn▮ crest, but mostly down, down, down, alternating dirt trail or stone steps. After you p▮ W005, a JUNCTION:

- **Tai Tam Tuk (the Lower Reservoir Path to Tai Tam Reservoir Road) — 1.3 k▮ 0.8 mi; 40 min — ahead — Hike 3D. Although not marked as such, this is ▮ way to the Wilson Trail and the Twins.**
- Wong Nai Chung Reservoir — 2.7 km/1.7 mi; 1 hr 30 min — right
- Unmarked — Tai Tam Reservoir — Upper Reservoir Path to Tai Tam Reserv▮ Road; about 45 min — left — Hike 3D
- Violet Hill — 1.1 km/0.7 mi; 45 min — back — Hike 3F

About 250 more steps down you arrive at another JUNCTION and signboard, w▮ CHOICES:

- **Wilson Trail/the Twins — cross the bridge over the catchwater and take ▮ stairs up to the right** — no distance shown but it is 2 km/1.2 mi (allow an h▮ unless you are very fit)
- Tai Tam Reservoir — cross the bridge over the catchwater and turn left to take ▮ Lower Reservoir Path to Tai Tam Reservoir Road; the signpost says "to Tai T▮ Tuk" — no distance shown but it is 1.3 km/0.8 mi; 40 min — Hike 3D.
- Repulse Bay — the unmarked trail to the right, and to the right of the Stanley W▮ Catchwater sign. It can be overgrown. The trail disgorges you at the Hong K▮ International School Elementary School campus in South Bay, after traversin▮ rocky streambed — about 30 mins.
- Stanley — follow the catchwater (Tsz Lo Lan Shan Path) to the right before ▮ bridge — about 3 km/1.8 mi; 30 min — Hike 3G

The signboard has a map of Section 1 of the Wilson Trail, Hike 3F. **There is ▮ emergency phone.**

If determined to tackle the Twins, take a deep breath, cross the bridge a▮ start up the stairs, passing marker W004. The trail climbs relentlessly up conc▮ stairs; be sure and stop to catch your breath and the views. You reach the top of the ▮ Twin (363 m) at marker W003. There are exhilarating views (enhanced, perhaps▮

cute lack of oxygen in your brain after that climb) of Kowloon, Chai Wan, Shek O, nd to the Peak, and everything in between.

After a break, start downhill, as the trail alternates with downhill stretches and uphill climbs, then begin your second big climb, not as long as the first one, to the second Twin (386 m) at marker W002. Take a well-earned break to enjoy the s and let your heart slow down.

The remaining 500 meters of trail is all steps down to Stanley Gap Road. The view s down on Stanley and Chung Hom Kok, and as you near the bottom, the trail is vertiginous, as it is exposed and steep. At marker W001, there is a view compass a map. When you are finished there, simply carry on down to the road.

To Continue to Hike

Chung Hom Kok — turn right at the road and walk a brief way to Chung Hom Kok Road, then down to the point of Chung Hom Kok Peninsula; see Hike 3K

To Leave the Trail

Stanley/Ma Hang — any bus that goes by will take you to Stanley, or you can walk there through Ma Hang from Chung Hom Kok Road, as above

Central or Parkview — buses No. 260, 6, 6X or 61 to Central; the 6 goes past Tai Tam Resevoir Road to Parkview.

Alternatives

To start from Chung Hom Kok, pick up the trail, marked by a large sign, on Stanley Gap Road about half-way between Chung Hom Kok and Stanley. There is a bus stop on Stanley Gap Road across from the trailhead.

You can reach the Twins from Parkview (Wong Nai Chung Gap) via Tai Tam Reservoir Road (Hike 3D) or Tsz Lo Lan Shan Path, Hike 3G.

3G TSZ LO LAN SHAN PATH AND CATCHWATER TO STANLEY ®

This is a alternative and more gentle route from Parkview to Repulse Bay Gap, where you can continue on an easy but very pretty trail to Stanley, or pick up the Twins or the Tai Tam Reservoir Upper or Lower Reservoir Paths; see Hikes 3F and 3D. A good part of the trail is a concrete catchwater; the rest is dirt and stone. In a few sections, the trail clings rather precariously to a hillside. It is tempting to recommend this hike for kids, as it is flat, but in many sections there is a steep drop off. Any children should be firmly attached to an adult. Much of the trail is suitable for running.

> Distance: 6 km/3.8 mi
> Difficulty: 1/5
> Time: 1 hr 30 min
> Rise: negligible
> Map 3.2 and 3.3
> Countryside Map Grid:
> • Start: 11 and 64
> • Finish: 12–13 and 60–
>   Repulse Bay Gap is jus
>   northwest of 12 and 62

To Get There

The trail begins at the Wong Nai Chung Reservoir, which is half way up Tai Tam Reser Road, between Parkview and Wong Nai Chung Gap Road. At the reservoir there map board showing the Tai Tam County Trail (Hike 3E) and the Tsz Lo Lan Shan F

Walk along the concrete path bordering the reservoir, and left along the reser dam, to a flight of stairs down along the dam wall, then left into the woods. A conc path trends upward, and shortly, a sign points left — **ignore this**, it marks the Tai Country Trail, Hike 3E. Keep going straight along the catchwater.

Follow the catchwater for about half an hour. You will pass over a few streaml and dams, in some cases with fewer railings than you might like. At one point, a se steps leads down: this detour takes you around a very narrow section of the catchwa There are not many views, but from time to time you will get a lovely glimpse of D Water Bay Mansions, Shouson Hill or Repulse Bay.

Eventually the catchwater becomes a dirt and rock trail that is primarily woo and shady, with the occasional exposed view-filled sections, curving along the hills There are very welcome railings in the most precipitous sections. The path can be ro in parts and muddy in parts, and leans slightly downhill. People do run this section, there's a fair risk for turning an ankle.

After a good view of South Bay and the Hong Kong International School Elemen School campus, you see the Twins ahead of you. Another few minutes, and the ends at an intersection with the Wilson Trail, just above Repulse Bay Gap, giving you several CHOICES:

- **Tai Tam Tuk (the Lower Reservoir Path to Tai Tam Reservoir Road) — 1.3 km/ 0.8 mi; 40 min — right — Hike 3D**
- Unmarked — Tai Tam Reservoir — Upper Reservoir Path to Tai Tam Reservoir Road — ahead — Hike 3D
- Violet Hill — 1.1 km/0.7 mi; 45 min — left — Hike 3F
- Wong Nai Chung Reservoir — 2.7 km/1.7 mi; 1 hr 30 min — back

After about 250 more steps down you arrive at another JUNCTION and signboard, with CHOICES:

- **Stanley — follow the catchwater to the right before the bridge — no distance is shown but it is about 3 km/1.8 mi; 30 min**
- Wilson Trail/the Twins — cross the bridge over the catchwater and take the stairs up to the right — no distance shown but it is 2 km/1.2 mi (allow an hour unless you are very fit)
- Tai Tam Reservoir — cross the bridge over the catchwater and turn left to take the Lower Reservoir Path to Tai Tam Reservoir Road; the signpost says "to Tai Tam Tuk" — no distance shown but it is 1.3 km/0.8 mi; 40 min — Hike 3D.
- Repulse Bay — the unmarked trail to the right, and to the right of the Stanley West Catchwater sign. It can be overgrown. The trail disgorges you at the Hong Kong International School Elementary School campus in South Bay, after traversing a rocky streambed — about 30 mins.

The signboard has a map of Section 1 of the Wilson Trail, Hike 3F. **There is an emergency phone**.

A concrete path about four feet wide parallels the catchwater, and as before, it is mostly in the woods with occasional views. The views you do get are marvelous ones. The catchment walls are marked with blue paint every 10 meters and sometimes with a little metal plaque. Near marker 1900 you are at the top of Chung Hom Kok Peninsula, curving around the hillside and then downhill to Stanley, with a beautiful view. By marker 3240 you are looking directly down at Stanley and just after 3320 the catchwater intersects with the Wilson Trail. Take the 300 or so steps down to the right (the catchwater continues, but only for a few meters.)

To Continue to Hike

Chung Hom Kok — turn right at Stanley Gap Road and walk a brief way to Chung Hom Kok Road, then down to the point of Chung Hom Kok Peninsula; see Hike 3K

To Leave the Trail

- Stanley/Ma Hang — any bus or minibus that goes by will take you to Stanley, or you can walk there through Ma Hang from Chung Hom Kok Road, as above.
- Central or Parkview — buses No. 260, 6, 6X or 61 to Central; the 6 goes past Tai Tam Resevoir Road to Parkview.

 Amenities

Wong Nai Chung Reservoir has a little snack bar and a pedal boat concession stand which open on weekends.

3H *LADY CLEMENTI'S RIDE*

Ⓚ Ⓝ Ⓡ

This hike has a bit of everything, stairs, flat sections, catchwaters, dirt, paving, open and tree covered sections, some interesting views, a Tree Walk, and a sense of history with some bunkers from World War II. The walk used to be a Bridle Path and is named after the wife of Sir Cecil Clementi, a former governor of Hong Kong. The lady had a reputation for being quite stuffy, even by the standards of the day. She would go to the library, located in what is now the Helena May, and rip out any pages of books that mentioned hugs or kisses. We imagine that book sales skyrocketed.

> Distance: 5.4 km/3.5 mi
> Difficulty: 2/5
> Time: 2 hr 30 min
> Rise: 170 m
> Ⓝ Maps 3.1
> Countryside Map Grid:
> Start: 10 and 64
> Finish: 08 and 65

The trail is suitable for running in many places, and a loop of upper and lower Lady Clementi's Ride makes a good run (about 4.4 km/2.75 mi round trip), although parts are a bit rocky and overgrown and you may need to slow down there.

Note: We here describe only a part of Lady Clementi's Ride. The full ride runs from Aberdeen Reservoir Road to Nam Fung Road, overlapping Hong Kong Trail Section 4 — Hike 2F.

To Get There:

From the gas station on Wong Nai Chung Gap Road, cross to the west side of Wong Nai Chung Gap Road, crossing the little park with the Order of Saint John Memorial. Go up the hill, then right (south) on Deep Water Bay Road. You have two options to access the trail: Black's Link or Nam Fung Road. The directions for Black's Link follow; the Nam Fung Road access is described below.

Immediately turn right on Black's Link Road. The road curves up past apartments and homes with views of the south side of the Island. After you pass the buildings, go past a gate. You will see the Aberdeen Country Park sign and then a Hong Kong Trail Distance Post, H049. At the huge electric pylon, look for a signpost:

Nam Fung Road (Lady Clementi's Ride) — left and down the stairs

Middle Gap (Black's Link) — ahead — Hike 2C

Wong Nai Chung Gap — back

No mileage is shown.)

Go down the steps under the power lines, staying to the left of the pylon. Take in brief but impressive views of the Hong Kong Golf Club and Deep Water Bay before you go into the tree-covered steps that go down and down. At the bottom of the stairs you will be just above Deep Water Bay Road. A signpost indicates that it is 0.4 km/0.25 mi back up the stairs to Black's Link. Turn right to ponder your CHOICES:

- Lady Clementi's Upper Ride — follow the catchwater, covered at this point with shady trees
- Lady Clementi's Lower Ride — after a few yards take the flight of steps to your left down to a dirt trail paralleling the catchwater at a lower level, then turn right. The trail is fairly flat until the end when it zigzags up the hill to the right to meet the Upper Ride and the catchwater. Beware of thorny plants and many spiders.

When the two trails rejoin, you may CHOOSE:

- **Follow the catchwater — ahead (left coming up from the Lower Ride)**
- Return along the alternate path, taking a right along the catchwater from the Lower Ride or a left into the woods from the Upper Ride (pick up the Lower Ride at slope registration sign 11SW DCR 801). (This makes a loop of about 4.4 km/2.75 mi.)

The trail suddenly widens; at first the bank on the left will be high enough to prevent views, but further along you have views of the southeast side of the Island including Ocean Park, Brick Hill and the road heading into the Aberdeen Tunnel. The trail diverges briefly, take the upper path to a JUNCTION (or the lower path to step right to the JUNCTION):

- **Aberdeen Upper Reservoir or Wan Chai Gap — ahead (no distance noted, see second Junction) — Hike 2E, Yellow Walk**
- To Black's Link via Middle Gap Road — 3.25 km/2 mi; 1 hr — back
- To Nam Fung Road via Lady Clementi's Ride — 2.75 km/1.7 mi; 45 min — back
- Aberdeen Lower Reservoir — 1.5 km/0.9 mi; 30 min — left — Hike 2E, Blue Walk

A short way uphill there is a second JUNCTION, which is also the intersection of the Yellow and Blue Walks of Aberdeen Country Park, see Hike 2E:

- **Wan Chai Gap (Lady Clementi's Ride) — 2.25 km/1.4 mi; 45 min — sharp right — Hike 2E, Yellow Walk**
- To Black's Link via Middle Gap Road — 3.25 km/2 mi; 1 hr — back
- Aberdeen Upper Reservoir — 1 km/0.6 mi; 15 min — right — Hike 2E, Blue Walk
- Aberdeen Lower Reservoir via Bennet's Hill — 1.5 km/0.9 mi; 30 min — straight ahead — Hike 2E, Blue Walk

There is a lovely rest stop here that looks out over Deep Water Bay, Ocean Park and Aberdeen. A perfect place to enjoy the view and have a (BYO) snack!

The Tree Walk signs begin here.

Cross over the catchwater and some falls that drain into Aberdeen Reservoir. After a series of steep stairs up, there is a small BBQ and picnic site and an old bunker from World War II on the right.

The trail now becomes a mostly dirt path with some rocky sections. The trees provide a welcome shade, as you cross several bridges and streams. A signpost reveals:

- **Wan Chai Gap — 1.25 km/0.8 mi; 30 min — ahead**
- Black's Link via Middle Gap Road — 4.25 km/2.6 mi; 1 hr 15 min — back

Both directions bear Yellow Walk tips — see Hike 2E.

Following the mostly flat trail, cross another bridge and an inviting deep pool of green water, then continue upward over rocky areas as the trail flattens out and crosses another stream with a lovely waterfall. Soon it turns into a narrow paved path and a JUNCTION:

- **Wan Chai Gap — 0.25 km/0.1 mi; 15 min — straight**
- Peel Rise to Wan Chai Gap (Hong Kong Trail Sections 4 and 3) — 5.75 km/3.5 mi; 1 hr 45 min — left
- Black's Link via Middle Gap Road (Hong Kong Trail Section 4) — 5 km/3.2 mi; 1 hr 30 min — back

Proceed forward up the slope and stairs until you reach Aberdeen Reservoir Road, which creates a JUNCTION:

Wan Chai Gap — 0.25 km/0.1 mi; 15 min — right
- Aberdeen Upper Reservoir — 1.5 km/0.9 mi; 30 min — left — the sign has the Yellow Walk tips; Hike 2E
- Black's Link via Lady Clementi's Ride and Magazine Gap Road — 5.25 km/3.3 mi; 1 hr 30 min — back

Walk up along the Aberdeen Reservoir Road, a short distance to Mount Cameron Road. Take a left and you will be at delightful Wan Chai Gap Park, Hub 2.

To Continue to Hike

Wan Chai Gap Green Trail to Wan Chai, or Bowen Road; see Hikes 2A, 2B

Black's Link back to your point of origin; see Hike 2C

Hong Kong Trail Section 3 in reverse to Peel Rise, see Hike 1L

To Leave the Trail

- Catch the No. 15 bus to Wan Chai and Central or take a taxi.

Directions from Nam Fung Road

From the gas station on Wong Nai Chung Gap Road, cross to the west side of the road, then cross the little park with the Order of Saint John Memorial. Go left up the hill, then right (south) on Deep Water Bay Road. Continue walking down Deep Water Bay Road and take the right fork onto Nam Fung Road. Across from the bus stop (marked "Nam Fung Road") there is a flight of about 8 steps with a sign, not visible from the road, for Lady Clementi's Ride. Take a left at the top of the stairs at the sign:

- **Lady Clementi's Lower Ride (unmarked) — ahead**
- Black's Link — right
- Nam Fung Road — back

Follow the Lower Ride as set forth above. You can also go right up a second set of stairs to reach the Upper Ride, turning left at the sign:

- **Lady Clementi's Upper Ride (unmarked) — left**
- Black's Link — 0.4 km/0.25 mi — up
- Nam Fung Road — back

 Alternatives

You may start Lady Clementi's Ride at Wan Chai Gap, Hub 2; see Hike 2E, Yellow Way from Wan Chai Gap or at Peel Rise, Hike 1L.

Note: *If you are hiking this trail in reverse, the lower trail diverges from the catchwater slope registration sign 11SW DCR 801 on the far side; just after sign 11SW D/F 1 on the trail side.*

3J REPULSE BAY SEAVIEW PROMENADE

Ⓓ Ⓚ Ⓡ Ⓢ

The Promenade is one of the few flat walks in Hong Kong. Combined with the Mills and Chung path, the walk goes all the way from Repulse Bay to the Hong Kong Country Club, just before Ocean Park. The views are magnificent, from close ups of boats and shore to long shots out over the bays to the shipping channel. Except for the stairs at either end, the walk is flat and perfect for jogging, strollers, family outings and people watching.

> Distance: 3.25 km/2 mi
> Difficulty: 1/5
> Time: 45 min
> Rise: negligible
> Ⓝ Map 3.3
> Countryside Map Grid:
> • Start: 11–12 and 61–62
> • Finish: 10–11 and 62–63

To Get There

By Bus:

Any No. 6 or 260 bus to Repulse Bay

No. 73 or 973 from Aberdeen to Repulse Bay

By Car:

Park at The Repulse Bay apartments, left just after the light; or take a left before The Repulse Bay apartments on Beach Road and park at meters along the road or in the little Dairy Farm lot at the end.

On Foot:

- From Stanley, Hike 3F in reverse (Difficulty: 5/5) or along the catchwater to Repulse Bay Gap; see Hike 3G, then down a rough trail; see Hike 3G

   From Wan Nai Chung Gap, any Hike to Repulse Bay Gap, such as 3E, 3F or 3G

From the bus stop at Repulse Bay, take the stairs down to the beach. Turn right and proceed along Beach Road to the Seaview Promenade and turn left. Alternatively, you could get off the bus at Beach Road, walk down under the overpass and turn right on the promenade.

As you turn on to the Seaview Promenade, look for a delightful little park on your left (the very northern end of Repulse Bay). Walk along the flat walkway and be sure to look back at the excellent view of the bay.

Note the large hole in the middle of The Repulse Bay apartments. According to some, the hole has a fung shui purpose, letting the "dragon energy" in the mountain get to the sea. Less spiritual observers note that it resembles a building in Miami, shown on "Miami Vice."

Walk behind a government building and head toward Deep Water Bay. There are always sailboats moored here and across the water, at the Hong Kong Yacht Club on Middle Island.

Pass a waterfall on the right, as well as the stairs up to the road and another bus stop. As you reach the beach area of Deep Water Bay, you have two CHOICES:

- **Mills and Chung Path — through the BBQ area (very popular on weekends) cross the sand to Island Road**
- leave the walk — take the stairs before the BBQ area to Island Road

If you decide to keep going, when you get to Island Road turn left along the sidewalk. The Hong Kong Golf Club is on your right, across the road. Pass the Victoria Racing Club on the left, to a set of stairs down that are clearly marked "Mills and Chung Path."

Enjoy more views of the channel and ships passing by. The path will end suddenly under a shady tree.

To Leave the Trail

- Take the stairs up to Island Road and the bus stop, Ocean Park and/or the Hong Kong Country Club.

Two Notable Sights

Before you start, or at the end of a round trip, visit the shrine at the far end (south) of Repulse Bay where you will find statues of Kwan Yin, the Goddess of Mercy, and Tin Hau, the fisherman's patron goddess, and many fanciful sculptures.

Amenities

There are several options for food, including McDonald's, KFC and Dominos in the Dairy Farm Shopping Center on the beach; Tai Fat Hau, a Chinese seafood restaurant on the waterfront; and a couple of upscale places in The Repulse Bay apartments. There are toilets in the beach bathhouses.

Alternatives

You might decide to walk only one way starting at Ocean Park; in that case, get off the bus at Shouson Hill Road. On the shore side of the road take the stairs down at the sign for the Mills and Chung Path.

3K CHUNG HOM KOK

Looking for a walk with great views but few tourists? Take a walk downhill to the end of the Chung Hom Kok Peninsula, partly on public road then on a road closed to all but local traffic. The end of the walk is the best part, as you travel along the point, with far reaching sea views and an old World War II bunker. This is a good one for a run and suitable for kids, especially if you walk down and bus or cab back up.

Distance: 3 km/1.9 mi
Difficulty: 1/5
Time: 45 min
Rise: 100 m
Map 3.3
Countryside Map Grid:
• Start: 11–12 and 60–61
• Finish: 11–12 and 58–59

To Get There

By Bus:

Take any No. 6 or 260 bus from Central, getting off at the bus stop just after you crest the hilltop coming out of Repulse Bay. There is a big sign for Stanley Plaza.

On Foot:

The trail can be accessed from the the Tsz Lo Lan Shan Path (Hike 3G), or the Twins (see Hike 3F) or by walking through Ma Hang from Stanley Plaza (see Hike 3L).

By Car:

There is a bit of space at the Dairy Farm Shopping Center on Chung Hom Kok Road. You could park in Stanley Plaza and walk up through Ma Hang.

Walk down Chung Hom Kok Road, or if you prefer, take the bus down, to a dead end roundabout. The road passes many townhouse complexes and has some nice views. Follow the signs for the Cheshire Home (a Hong Kong Jockey Club nursing home) along a paved road that sees little traffic except to the home. The road curves along the coast, and at the end takes you to some picnic sites at the tip of the peninsula, with sea views — once we saw a ray in the water here. The Countryside Map shows a cave of the famous Qing Dynasty Pirate Cheung Po Tsai, but we have not searched for it. (Almost every cave in Hong Kong seems to be a Cheung Po Tsai Cave, sort of a "George Washington slept here" syndrome.)

On the way back, consider a detour up Cape Road to Ma Hang, and the beautiful Kwan Yin Temple. From there you can walk down to Stanley Plaza, where you can find lots of bars, restaurants and shops. Either walk along Cape Road, or for a back way, take the stairs to the right of the Kwan Yin Temple gate, next to the Cape Road bus stop.

After climbing about 55 steps, you will descend 195 or so more steps to Stanley, through jungle-like woods (5 to 10 minutes). When you reach the bottom of the steps, turn left about 0.2 km (0.1 mile) to Murray House. If you are not pressed for time, before going left to Murray House, turn right to visit the Pak Tai Temple, only a few feet away.

L STANLEY FORT

Ⓡ Ⓢ Ⓒ

w tourists get past Stanley Market, but this hike takes along the peninsula for unique views and some history ell. A long pull uphill on a public road, the hike is not for a run. The road has good sidewalks in the inning and not much traffic when the sidewalks peter although the busses and construction trucks do zoom There are pretty views of the sea and Stanley. You can and rest at the peaceful Stanley Military Cemetery, aining many colonial and World War II graves. When get to the People's Liberation Army Fort (the old ley Fort) your only option, like the Grand Old Duke ork, is to march your men back down again.

Distance: 1.5 km/0.9 mi
Difficulty: 2/5
Time: 30 min
Rise: 120 m
🧭 Map 9
Countryside Map Grid:
• Start: 12–13 and 59–60
• Finish: 13 and 57–58

To Get There

Bus:
 No. 6 bus or 260 from Central to Stanley
 973 from Aberdeen to Stanley

Foot:
m Parkview; see Hike 3G

Car:
re is parking on Stanley Beach Road but it does tend to fill quickly on weekends.
re is also parking at Stanley Plaza.

he Stanley bus terminus (not Stanley Plaza), walk along Stanley Main Road South the post office and police station. At the fork in the road, take the right fork, Wong Kok Road.

Wong Ma Kok Road passes the back of St. Stephen's College on the left, then down up a small hill. Next, it runs down between Stanley Military Cemetery and the back tanley Prison on the left, a school and the road to St. Stephen's Beach on the right. v you face the long climb uphill. Once you pass the water treatment plant on the looking like something out of a James Bond movie, there is one development about -way up. There are a few stray dogs (see "What You Should Know").

The views of the sea are lovely here and, apart from the buses, the road is quiet the top, Stanley Fort, now occupied by the PLA, is as far as you can go. You must t around and go back down. If you are lucky the armed guard will give you a wave, usually they are impassive. Going downhill you can enjoy pretty views of Stanley Now go get that well-earned beer on the beach front.

Worthwhile Side Trips

Stop off at the cemetery, which is beautifully kept and quiet. If the chapel at S Stephen's College is open you can peek in to see the stained glass window commemorat the World War II Stanley Internment. To get there, go through the sport fields climb up to the main campus.

Stanley has many temples, and a visit to one of the lesser known ones, the Pak Temple, makes a nice little excursion. Go to the far end of Murray House, and arou the end, to a pair of stone pillars framing a path. The path leads under a banyan overhang to the little temple on the seaside. The stairs that you pass on the right lea the Kwan Yin Temple on Cape Road in Ma Hang, which is also worth a visit. It's ano 10-minute walk along a woodsy path, up about 195 steps.

3M *TAI TAM TREE WALK* Ⓚ Ⓝ

A sweet little path branching off from Tai Tam Reservoir Road just inside the park, this is a winner with kids. Markers identify trees and plants as the trail winds through BBQ area.

> Distance: 0.1 km/0.06 mi
> Difficulty: 1/5
> Time: 15 min
> Rise: negligible
> Ⓝ Map 3.2
> Countryside Map Grid:
> 12 and 64

▶ To Get There

From Wong Nai Chung Gap walk up Tai Tam Reservoir Road to Parkview. Beyond the entrance to Parkview, as the road turns downhill, there is a gate and sign for Tai Tam Country Park.

At marker T8201, the paved road heads down the hill, past a picnic site on the left and a BBQ site on the right, a clue to the popularity of the area for family outings on weekends and public holidays. Toilet facilities can be found on the left as well as a second BBQ site. Further down the road, across from the Agricultural Building, is the Tai Tam Tree Walk on the right, passing up through BBQ site No. 3. It's short and sweet but a good excuse to get the kids (or yourself) out for a little excursion, education and picnic.

3N WONG NAI CHUNG TREE WALK

This walk, good for kids, provides surprisingly good views from a fairly level path, which is also a Tree Walk. The trail overlaps Sir Cecil's Ride until it reaches Mount Butler Road; see Hike 3C.

> Distance: 2 km/1.25 mi
> Difficulty: 1/5
> Time: 1 hr
> Rise: negligible
> Map 3.2
> Countryside Map Grid:
> • Start and Finish:
>   10–11 and 64
>   (not marked as a Tree Wal[k]
>   on the Countryside Map)

To Get There

Take the stairs just uphill from the gas station on Wong Nai Chung Gap Road and ma[ke] an immediate left turn. If you are coming down Tai Tam Reservoir Road, either take t[he] path to the right between the bridge and the little park, or the steps just beyond the [car] park driveway. At our last visit, the signboard at the top of these steps had a sha[rk] warning poster — you just aren't safe anywhere in Hong Kong! At the bottom of t[he] stairs, you will see a map board, and a Tree Walk marker.

Follow the lovely, flat, tree-lined dirt walk past several plant identification mark[ers] as it winds around some apartment buildings.

Pass marker C4109 in back of the Cricket Club, soon arriving at a picnic s[ite] overlooking the club grounds and Mount Nicholson (430 m). **An emergency phone [is] nearby**.

After another picnic area and a concrete shelter that has tables and benches, foll[ow] a rock-paved path to a JUNCTION:

- **Tree Walk — ahead**
- Tai Hang Road (Happy Valley) — steps down to the left
- Parkview — right, up steep steps. Cross over a covered reservoir, then up m[ore] stairs to a catchwater; turn right to Tai Tam Reservoir Road

Shortly, you will arrive at a second JUNCTION and a signpost:

- **Mount Butler Road — 0.8 km/0.5 mi; 15 min — ahead**
- Parkview (Tai Tam Country Trail) — steps to the right; see Hike 3E.
- Tai Hang Road (Happy Valley) —stairs down to the left
- Tai Tam Reservoir Road — 1.6 km/1 mi; 30 min — back

As you continue, you pass more sets of stairs going downhill to Tai Hang Road. Shortly, you reach a stone marker indicating "Home Affairs Dept. Project" on the right. There is a red urn here and Chinese characters inscribed in the wall; red poles form an entrance that leads up to well-tended gardens. If you reach this point in the morning, you will probably find people playing mahjong and practicing Tai Chi. There is a **telephone** next to the gate.

Back along the main path, follow concrete steps with dirt on either side, across some streambeds. The path turns right as you head up the stairs. You soon reach a JUNCTION:

- **Tree Walk — left**
- To explore a lovely group of well-kept shrines — straight and up stairs.

You are still following the Tree Walk, crossing more streams before taking stairs down to the left to Mount Butler Road and your CHOICES:

To Continue to Hike

- Return along the Tree Walk
  Continue on Sir Cecil's Ride; see Hike 3C.

To Leave the Trail

Just after a signpost reading "Wong Nai Chung Tree Walk — 2 km," a set of stairs to the left leads to the intersection of Mount Butler and Henderson Roads and a bus stop for minibus No. 24 to Admiralty or bus No. 11 to Central Pier/Admiralty.

QUARRY GAP

..lthough somewhat of a challenge to get to, this hub rewards the hiker with energetic
..es and super views. Mount Parker Road (not accessible to cars) runs north/south or
..ough the gap, intersecting Tai Tam Reservoir Road. Thus, while Quarry Gap (Tai
..g Au in Chinese) is the hub, the access points are Quarry Bay and Tai Tam. Many of
..Hub 3 hikes end up in Quarry Gap, such as 3A, 3B, and 3C. You can start in Quarry
..; include some hikes at Tai Tam Reservoir, and finish in or near Stanley or at Parkview.
..Extended Hikes in the Appendices.

Map 4

..untryside Map Grid: 12–13 and 65

..e: *Mileages and times listed do not include getting to the trail head.*

To Get There

MTR:

..nd Line to Tai Koo, Exit B. Turn left on King's Road, and left again on Greig Road or
..Mount Parker Road just before the raised walkway (there is a sign posted on a fake
..: but it's hard to see among the clutter of other signs). Mount Parker Road runs
..ill about 3 km/1.9 mi and will take about 45 minutes to walk up to the gap; see Hike

Bus:

..ong others, No. 2 or 720 from Exchange Square to Tai Koo MTR

..m the south side, minibus No. 6 from Stanley to Chai Wan, then MTR to Tai Koo

Car:

..:re is parking at Cityplaza on Tai Fung Avenue, and at Grand Plaza next to Tai Koo
..R. There is also a parking lot at Devon House, Taikoo Place, Quarry Bay.

Foot:

..m Tai Tam Road, Tai Tam Reservoir Road, or Mount Parker Road; see Hikes 3D and

4A HONG KONG TRAIL SECTION 6 — QUARRY GAP TO TAI TAM ROAD Ⓡ

The most difficult part of this hike is getting to it. From Quarry Gap, Mount Par
Road runs steadily downhill, following along the banks of the reservoirs. It then becom
a path, wandering through shaded and wooded areas, and crossing over a few strea
and waterfalls, ending at Tai Tam Road. While not the most spectacular of hikes, it
good way to connect the many trails in this area, and a good workout if done in rever
which is mostly uphill.

Distance: 4.5 km/2.8 mi	Difficulty: 1/5	Time: 1 hr 30 min
Rise: 370 m	Map 4	
Countryside Map Grid: • Start: 12–13 and 65 • Finish: 13–14 and 63		

4B MOUNT PARKER ROAD TO BOA VISTA HILL Ⓕ Ⓡ Ⓢ Ⓜ

Climb out of Quarry Bay on steep but paved Mount Parker Road to a scenic, fa
easy, tree-shaded trail. The road has some lovely views of the city. The trail, runn
south from Quarry Gap to Boa Vista Hill (260 m), has some excellent views: first to
west, including the reservoirs; then to the east, over Victoria Harbor; and finally to
south, including Tai Tam Harbor. The last mile of the hike is a road that gently slo
downhill before returning to Mount Parker Road, and is suitable for jogging.

Distance: 6.5 km/4 mi	Difficulty: 3/5	Time: 2 hr 30 min
Rise: 300 m	Map 4	
Countryside Map Grid: • Start: 12–13 and 67 • Finish: 13–14 and 63–64		

4C HONG PAK COUNTRY TRAIL Ⓚ Ⓢ Ⓢ Ⓜ

A jewel of a trail, this trek curves in and out of the canyons above Tai Koo Shi
The views are far too good for such an easy hike and encompass the entire eastern
of Victoria Harbor. The trail is a big loop starting and ending on Mount Parker Ro
about 2 km/1.2 mi up from Tai Koo. A good trail for kids, it has boulders to climb o
and streams to cross, and is not too demanding.

Distance: 3.6 km/2.2 mi	Difficulty: 2/5	Time: 1 hr 45 min
Rise: 200 m	Map 4	
Countryside Map Grid : • Start: 12–13 and 67 • Finish: 12–13 and 66–67		

QUARRY BAY TREE WALK 🄺 🄽 🅈

This is a unique section of the Wilson Trail: a Tree Walk, ruins from World War II, a Morning Walkers' Garden are all tucked into the trees not far from Kornhill. A rt pleasant outing with some Hong Kong history as a bonus.

Distance: 1.1 km/0.7 mi	Difficulty: 2/5	Time: 30 min
Rise: 100 m	Map 4	
Countryside Map Grid: • Start: 12–13 and 66 • Finish: 12–13 and 66–67		

Hub Amenities

arry Gap has toilets and a small fitness area. There are also toilets, a restaurant, and market at Parkview. Stores, bakeries, and restaurants are easily found along King's d, including a Wellcome at Quarry Bay MTR. Tai Koo MTR Station has several rs of shops and restaurants. From Tai Tam Reservoir Road, you have a choice of ley or Chai Wan, both accessible by minibus, for transit hubs and amenities.

Map 4 4A 4B 4C 4D

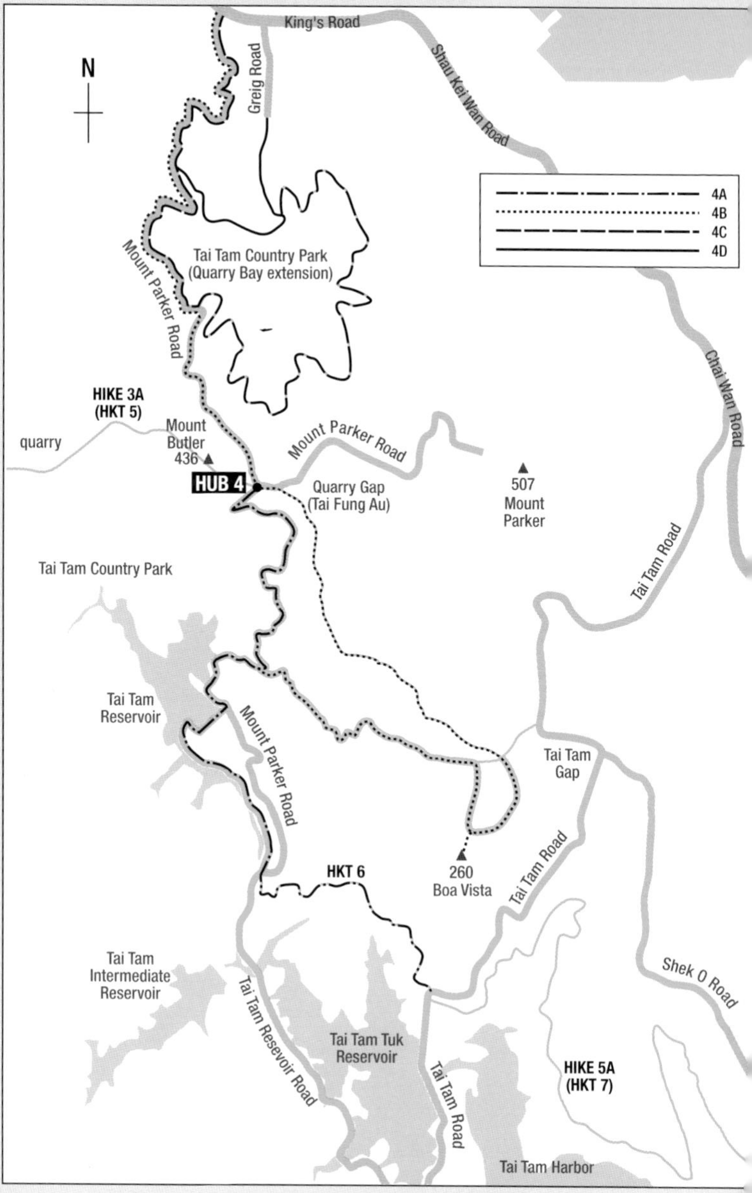

4A

HONG KONG TRAIL SECTION 6 — QUARRY GAP TO TAI TAM ROAD

Ⓡ

Not the most scenic section of the Hong Kong Trail, section 6 is an easy walk (in this direction) and a good way to get from Quarry Gap to Tai Tam. The trail travels downhill along Mount Parker Road and Tai Tam Reservoir Road, around the Tai Tam Reservoirs, and then through some wooded areas crossing several streams, ending up at Tai Tam Road near the reservoir dam. In reverse, this climb up Mount Butler (436 m) is a popular training hike or run, with a difficulty rating of 5/5.

> Distance: 4.5 km/2.8 mi
> Difficulty: 1/5
> Timing: 1 hr 30 min
> Rise: 370 m
> 🚩 Map 4
> Countryside Map Grid:
> Start: 12–13 and 65
> Finish: 13–14 and 63

▶ To Get There

Follow the Hub directions to Quarry Gap. Looking at the map board at Quarry Gap, take Mount Parker Road downhill to the right.

You will shortly pass marker H060. The road is paved and wide, and runs relentlessly downhill, passing over streams and in and out of open and wooded areas. There are some views, including a very nice one at the beginning, but in most areas the shrubbery is too high. Near the Tai Tam County Park entrance, there are numerous BBQ and picnic sites.

Look up at the hills above as you steadily descend, and at a view of the Redhill Peninsula you round the turn after marker H062. Just after a picnic area, a JUNCTION:

Tai Tam Reservoir — 0.75 km/0.5 mi; 15 min — straight
Unmarked — Boa Vista Hill, left along the paved road — Hike 4B
Mount Butler — 1.35 km/0.8 mi; 45 min — back

Take Mount Parker Road to the bottom of the hill and the reservoir dam. The trail to the left is the continuation of Mount Parker Road and meets the trail again further down, near marker H065. At the dam, there is a marker pointing out the Hong Kong Trail (back) and a sign for Tai Tam Upper Reservoir (also back). **Cross the dam.**

On the far side of the dam, a sign advises:
Hong Kong Trail — right
Tai Tam Upper Reservoir — back
Unmarked — left — also leads to the Hong Kong Trail; both directions simply carry you around either side of a small hill
(no mileage is shown.)

We will be purists and follow the trail to the right. Round the hill along the reservoir coming to another dam and a signpost at a JUNCTION:

- **Tai Tam Road — 1.75 km/1.1 mi; 45 min — ahead**
- Mount Butler — 2 km/1.25 mi; 1 hr — back; see Hikes 4B and 3A.
- Tai Tam Country Park Management Center — 0.75 km/0.5 mi; 15 min — right

Note: Signs are posted in the area to warn visitors that violent floods can occur suddenly without warning.

If you came to Hong Kong Trail Section 6 from Parkview, going down Tai Tam Reservoir Road, you will connect to the trail at this point; See Hike 3D.

Continue walking. Almost immediately, there is another dam — this is where the trails around the hill meet:

- **Hong Kong Trail — Tai Tam Road — right**
- Hong Kong Trail — Wong Nai Chung Gap Road — left

(No mileage is shown.)

Cross the dam and walk along the road. There are several picnic and BBQ areas on the left. Note the 3-sided concrete obelisk, probably a boundary marker, now too eroded to read. Keep to the paved path until you reach two JUNCTIONS:

- **Tai Tam — Hong Kong Trail (Section 7) — 1 km/0.6 mi; 30 min — left up the stairs** (the time is exaggerated, 15 min or less is more accurate)
- Tai Tam Tuk Reservoir (Tai Tam Road) — 1.75 km/1 mi; 30 min — ahead

and

- Mount Parker Road — left
- Tai Tam Reservoir — 0.75 km/0.5 mi; 30 min — back (again the time is exaggerated perhaps because of the steep hill)

When we last hiked this trail, marker T8205 had been uprooted and was waiting for replanting; it should now be somewhere in the vicinity.

Climb up the stairs (but not the concrete flight, which is for maintenance) and then up and down through scrawny pines along a path (muddy if it has rained recently).

At marker H066 the path trails through a canopy of trees with vines hanging down all around. You may hear many birds singing. Just as you feel you are going down too far, you cross a stream on a wooden platform, and then go up and down, crossing more streams. Continuing through this wooded area, you will hear the roar of cars before you go up the stairs and abruptly come out on Tai Tam Road. Watch out for wild dogs in the area, but they are usually not hostile.

To Continue to Hike

Continue across Tai Tam Road on Hong Kong Trail Section 7 — Hike 5A

Return to Tai Tam Reservoir Road along Tai Tam Bay. Cross Tai Tam Road, turn right, and take a concrete path to the left just before the huge dam. The path will take you down to the water (Tai Tam Bay). Turn right and follow the path below the dam and past some abandoned village homes. The trail follows along the side of the water, and ends up on Tai Tam Reservoir Road at the back of the Hong Kong International School Middle School campus. Go up Tai Tam Reservoir Road to Tai Tam Road. You will see the entrance to Tai Tam Country Park for a return walk to Parkview or Quarry Gap; see Hike 3D. (In theory, you could walk across the dam on Tai Tam Road, but this is not recommended as it is too narrow for the traffic it bears.)

To Leave the Trail

ou have had enough for the day, there is a bus stop just down the road to your right. can catch a bus to nearby Stanley and visit the Stanley market or one of the many aurants there for a good lunch. You can also flag down a minibus to Chai Wan, re you can find amenities and the MTR.

4B MOUNT PARKER ROAD TO BOA VISTA HILL

F D R S M

Boa Vista Hill (260 m) lies to the east of the Tai Tam Reservoirs within Tai Tam Country Park. The 3.5 km/ 2.2 mi trail travels along a rocky, downward-sloping path, and offers some charming views of both the reservoirs to the west and Chai Wan to the east, as it swings back toward Mount Parker Road, then climbs the short distance to the top of Boa Vista for fabulous views to the south. This route takes you up Mount Parker Road, itself a good uphill hike (3 km/1.9 mi), to Quarry Gap (Tai Fung Au), where you can pick up the path to Boa Vista Hill. The trail has sections that are suitable for running.

Distance: 6.5 km/4 mi
Difficulty: 3/5
Time: 2 hr 30 min
Rise: 300 m
Map 4
Countryside Map Grid:
• Start: 12–13 and 67
• Finish: 13–14 and 63–6

 To Get There

See Hub directions to Mount Parker Road. Take Mount Parker Road uphill passing B sites, picnic areas, and toilet facilities. On weekends, you'll find families out in force enjoy a picnic. We have even seen people hauling small toy wagons full of BBQ briquet up the hill for the festivities.

You will first see a few stands where sodas and snacks are sold. Pass them and y will leave the town behind. The road curves past an old mansion, Woodside Hou Further up the hill, steps to the right lead to a Morning Walkers' Garden. Conservancy Association has posted signs with environmental information. Turn arou occasionally to catch some excellent views of the city.

Pass several signs for Sir Cecil's Ride, each pointing up the stairs to the right; Hike 3C. After about 1 km/0.6 mi, a well-marked sign on the left points out the Qua Bay Tree Walk (also part of the Wilson Trail Section 2) to Quarry Bay, Hike 4D. A sh distance later, the Wilson Trail towards Parkview (Wong Nai Chung Gap) climbs p the pavilion up to the right. (This path also leads to Sir Cecil's Ride and the Quarry Jogging Trail, Hike 3C.)

Keep climbing up Mount Parker Road and you will reach the official beginni end of Sir Cecil's Ride, Hike 3C. There is a map board with an orienteering course.

Up about 2 km/1.2 mi from the start, there is a service road downhill to the left for the Tai Tam Country Park (Quarry Bay Extension), which leads to the Hong Pak Country Trail, Hike 4C.

Finally, you reach Quarry Gap and these CHOICES:

- **Boa Vista Trail — left up Mount Parker Road**
- Wong Nai Chung Gap via Mount Butler (Hong Kong Trail Section 5) — 4 km/ 2.5 mi; 1 hr 30 min — right — Hike 3A
- Tai Tam Tuk Reservoir (Hong Kong Trail Section 6) — 4.5 km/2.8 mi; 1 hr 30 min — down the hill to the right — Hike 4A
- Quarry Bay — 3 km/1.9 mi; 40 min — back

Proceed up Mount Parker Road towards the wireless transmitting station. A short distance up on the right, you will see a small sign for Boa Vista Hill and a dirt trail leading off to the right.

The dirt trail begins as a flat and fairly smooth path as it heads south under a protective canopy of trees. Becoming more rocky, it curves to the left around the hill, and begins a continuous, but gentle, descent. After crossing a stream, look for a bench to the left; you can take a brief rest here to take in reservoir views to the west. A short distance down the trail and opposite the Tai Tam Intermediate Reservoir is a second bench. It also overlooks far-reaching views, including one of Repulse Bay Gap in the distance.

Continue down the rocky path, walking under power lines, to suddenly arrive at an open, flat, grassy area. There are unusual views to the east of Chai Wan: the huge cemeteries (Buddhist, Muslim, Roman Catholic, Chinese, and Sai Wan War Cemetery) of Shau Kei Wan, Pottinger Peak (312 m) on the eastern tip of Hong Kong Island, and High Junk Peak in Kowloon. Head down through high shrubs to a catchwater and a JUNCTION:

Tai Tam Reservoir — forward

Tai Tam Road — just past the catchwater, a sign in Chinese and English on the left marks a path down to Tai Tam Road; it connects to Tai Tam Road just north of the roundabout at Tai Tam Gap (Shek O Peninsula). Countryside Map Grid 14–15 and 64.

Tai Fung Au (Quarry Gap) — back

Continue up the dirt road as it bends right and then down to a flat clearing and the beginning of the paved road. A sign notes:

Tai Fung Au (Quarry Gap) — 1.8 km/1.1 mi; 45 min — back

As the paved road curves down, stairs to the left lead to the top of Boa Vista, a trigonometric station and a view bonanza. From the south to the west, you can see Tai Tam Harbor and Red Hill Peninsula, as well as the Tai Tam Reservoirs and Repulse Bay

CHOICES:
- Tai Tam Reservoir — 0.75 km/0.6 mi; 15 min — return to Mount Parker Road downhill.
- Mount Butler — 1.25 km/0.75 mi; 45 min — also return to Mount Parker Road then uphill from Quarry Gap — Hike 3A

 ## To Continue to Hike
- Down Mount Parker Road to Tai Tam Reservoir Road, Hike 4A. From Tai Tam Reservoir Road you can continue up to Parkview, or take the Upper or Lower Reservoir Trail to Repulse Bay Gap, Hike 3D.
- Back to the Quarry Gap Hub for Hikes 3A, 3B or 3C; in reverse, 4A or 4C.

 ## To Leave the Trail
- Up Mount Parker Road to Quarry Gap and on to Quarry Bay
- Down Mount Parker Road to Tai Tam Reservoir Road and on to Tai Tam Road

 ## Alternatives
Any hike into Quarry Gap will take you to the start of the Boa Vista Trail (skipping Mount Parker Road); see Hikes 3A and 3C.

C HONG PAK COUNTRY TRAIL

Ⓚ Ⓜ Ⓢ Ⓧ

[N]ot well-known, this very scenic trail contours in and
[out] of the canyons high up behind Kornhill, just below
[Qu]arry Gap. There are much better views than you would
[exp]ect (or deserve) for a relatively easy hike. The walk is
[one] of contrasts with views of dense city below you. Kids
[wil]l like this one, as there are boulders to clamber over
[and] streams to cross.

> Distance: 3.6 km/2.2 mi
> Difficulty: 2/5
> Time: 1 hr 45 min
> Rise: 200 m
> 🧭 Map 4
> Countryside Map Grid:
> • Start: 12–13 and 67
> • Finish: 12–13 and 66–67

To Get There

[Foll]ow the Hub directions to Mount Parker Road and turn left.

Climb up Mount Parker Road about 2 km/1.2 mi to a paved road that heads sharply
[dow]nhill to the east. You can't miss the very large sign for Tai Tam Country Park (Quarry
[Bay Extension). Go down the service road a very short distance to a map board (on the
[righ]t), which has a detailed map of Hong Pak Country Trail. A sign for Kornhill points
[righ]t. The trail is marked with C distance markers at regular intervals.

The trail begins on a flat dirt path in an area densely covered by trees. The first part
[esta]blishes a repeating theme: the trail heads into a canyon, then crosses over a stream
[(or streams) on concrete or rock bridges, and moves back out of the canyon. With each
[suc]cessive canyon, the views spread wider and wider until you have a sweeping view of
[the] harbor, all the way from High Junk Peak in the east to the old Kai Tak airport site in
[the] north.

The trail has many flat sections, interspersed with stairs, as it contours below Mount
[But]ler and Mount Parker; it is mostly dirt, but one section is particularly rocky. There
[are] many boulders and it is fun to go in, out, and around them. At one point as the trail
[cro]sses over the top of an enormous boulder, you can hear a stream running underneath.
[Sho]rtly after this point, you descend stairs, cross a bridge, and pass marker C4303.

You will pass many markers that note Kornhill ahead and Mount Parker Road
[beh]ind. Some of these seem to be there to confirm any doubts that you are on the right
[trai]l; some of them block old paths off the trail.

After some stairs up to a flat section, then down again past another set of Kornhill/
[Mo]unt Parker Road signs, you enter an area near marker C4304 where the trail is very
[flat], the dirt is very red, and there are many pine trees. Note the erosion on the right side

of the hill. Directly across the small canyon to your left, you can see a very large boul
with a mysterious face. Is it a cat? fish? buffalo?

The trail curls around the hill and then heads northeast through a small gap. Th
are more views of the harbor. After some stairs, boulders and a stream, you reach a
section before heading to a small JUNCTION:

- **Kornhill — ahead**
- Mount Parker Road — back

Detour to the right along the chain-link fence to reach an enormous boulder
equally enormous views.

Back on the trail, head down the stairs along the chain-link fence, past mar
C4305. After yet more stairs, the trail becomes flat as you head under the trees. M
different sets of stairs lead you down to a flat dirt landing. Signs indicate:

- **Morning Walkers' Garden — left**
- Hung Tung Estate — straight
- Mount Parker Road — back

Now that you need a sign for Kornhill, after passing so many unnecessary or
there is no mention of it! Go left down the steep steps towards the Morning Walk
Garden. After many flat dirt areas, concrete stairs lead down to the now welcome si

- **Kornhill — left**
- Mount Parker Road — back

At C4306, pass two more Kornhill/Mount Parker Road signs and another strea
and the trail takes you to a lovely, large shelter; a nice place to take a break in the sha

Go down the stairs to yet another Kornhill/Mount Parker Road sign. There wil
a series of broad, sloping steps that zigzag down the hill to the end of the trail and
junction with the Quarry Bay Tree Walk (Wilson Trail), Hike 4D.

CHOICES:

- **Wilson Trail to Quarry Bay — right**
- Wilson Trail to Wong Nai Chung Reservoir via Quarry Gap — ahead — Hikes
  3C
- Mount Parker Road (Hong Pak Country Trail — 3.6 km/2.2 mi; 1 hr 45 min
  Hike 4C) — back (it is much faster to go ahead to get to Mount Parker Road.)

There is a map board of the Hong Pak Country Trail.

Follow the catchwater, which must have been a charming stream before it was
ered with concrete, to a paved area with a bench, a map board showing the Wilson
l, a sign for the Quarry Bay Country Park, and a marble marker that says "The
son Trail Tai Koo Section."

Cross the paved area and turn left down the stairs and along a concrete path in
t of a very large apartment complex. Pass W018 as you reach the exit at Greig Road.
ow Greig Road downhill to King's Road and turn right to reach the MTR (Tai Koo
ion).

Alternatives

hike into Quarry Gap will take you to Mount Parker Road; see Hikes 3A and 3C.
k down the road to the trail entrance at the Quarry Bay Management Center, Tai
Country Park.

4D QUARRY BAY TREE WALK

Ⓚ Ⓝ Ⓢ

A tree-shaded visit with nature and history, this walk can stand alone for a short outing, or as an add-on at the end of another hike, such as Sir Cecil's Ride, Hike 3C. Either way, it's a pleasant surprise that is hidden almost in the heart of the city. Kids will enjoy this one, too.

Distance: 1.1 km/0.7 mi
Difficulty: 2/5
Time: 30 min
Rise: 100 m
 Map 4
Countryside Map Grid:
• Start: 12–13 and 66
• Finish: 12–13 and 66–6

🢂 To Get There

The trail is very clearly marked by a Tree Walk gate on Mount Parker Road about 0.8 0.5 mi up from Quarry Bay. It overlaps the last part of Section 2 of the Wilson Trail, is marked with W distance markers; see Hike 3B.

Proceed down the stairs, and then up and past an old ruin. It is not identified might have been a wartime storeroom. At marker W017, look for the outdoor v stoves built as public kitchens in 1938–39. These were intended to feed people displa from their homes by the impending Japanese invasion. Since the battles lasted on few days, the kitchens were never used.

Follow the path as it heads up some stairs to another public kitchen. A Morn Walkers' Garden is signed to the right. The Tree Walk continues to the left through north side of this second kitchen, down a series of stairs past a picnic table, and ac a bridge over a stream. Soon you reach the Kornhill BBQ site and a sign:

• **Kornhill — forward**
• Tai Fung Au (Quarry Gap) — back

Pass the flat paved area that holds a shelter and more remnants of the public kitche as well as some play equipment. Then go down the stairs to another BBQ site ar JUNCTION:

• **Wilson Trail to Quarry Bay — left**
• Mount Parker Road (Hong Pak Country Trail — 3.6 km/2.25 mi; 1 hr 45 mir Hike 4C) — ahead (it is much faster to go back to Mount Parker Road.)
• Wilson Trail to Wong Nai Chung Reservoir via Quarry Gap — back — Hikes 3C

There is a map board showing the Hong Pak Country Trail, Hike 4C.

Follow the catchwater, which must have been a charming stream before it was ered with concrete, to a paved area with a bench, a map board showing the Wilson il, a sign for the Quarry Bay Country Park, and a marble marker that says "The son Trail Tai Koo Section."

Cross the paved area and turn left down the stairs and along a concrete path in it of a very large apartment complex. Pass W018 as you reach the exit at Greig Road. low Greig Road downhill to King's Road and turn right to reach the MTR (Tai Koo ion).

SHEK O PENINSULA (TAI TAM GAP)

ıek O, a remote peninsula on the south side, has three of the Island's most scenic
popular hikes, including the famous Dragon's Back. There are plenty of sea views,
ıto-pop singers' mansions, paragliders, and seaside villages. This hub is a bit spread
so directions to the start are also contained in each hike description.

Map 5

ıntryside Map Grid: 14–15 and 64 (Tai Tam Gap).
village of Shek O is at 16–17 and 60–61.

To Get There

Bus/MTR:

MTR to Shau Kei Wan; bus No. 9 towards Shek O

MTR to Chai Wan and minibus No. 16M towards Stanley to Tai Tam Gap (Shek O
Roundabout)

Bus No. 260 or any 6 to Stanley; minibus No. 16 M from Stanley towards Chai Wan

Foot:

Hong Kong Trail Section 6 from Tai Tam or Quarry Gap, see Hike 4A

From Chai Wan; see Hike 5C

Tai Tam Road and Shek O Road are not recommended for walking.

Car:

weekdays or very early on a weekend, there is parking available at Big Wave Bay and
ık O; however, at Big Wave Bay, it is metered with a two-hour limit. It may soon
ome the same at Shek O. There are a few parking spots above To Tei Wan on Shek O
ıd. Otherwise, it is best to park in Stanley or Chai Wan and take a bus over. You can
by taxi also but it will be expensive.

5A HONG KONG TRAIL SECTION 7 — TAI TAM ROAD TO TO TEI WAN 🅢🅟

This section of the Hong Kong Trail is exceptionally flat, until the end, whic
exceptionally steep! After a dull start, the trail has long sweeps of views from Tai T
Harbor to Stanley. It follows along a catchwater until it reaches the tiny village of To
Wan and the "Hobie Cat Beach." Be prepared for a seemingly endless procession
stairs from there up to Shek O Road.

Distance: 7.5 km/4.7 mi	Difficulty: 1/5 plus 5/5 stairs	Time: 2 hr
Rise: 250 m	Maps 4 and 5	
Countryside Map Grid: • Start: 13–14 and 63 • Finish: 15–16 and 60–61		

5B HONG KONG TRAIL SECTION 8 (DRAGON'S BACK)— TO TEI WAN TO
WAVE BAY 🅢 🆂🅲

Dragon's Back is one of the most scenic sections of the Hong Kong Trail. The
goes up and down along the spine of the peninsula, which from a distance looks li
dragon's back. The views are deservedly famous, stretching in all directions, and incl
a bird's-eye view of some very fancy mansions. This is a popular trail, and many pe
bring their kids along, though it is not an easy climb. We offer some easier short c

Distance: 8.5 km/5.3 mi	Difficulty: 4/5	Time: 2 hr 30 min
Rise: 312 m	Map 5	
Countryside Map Grid: • Start: 15–16 and 60–61 • Finish: 16–17 and 62–63		
The trail travels north to a U-turn at 14–15 and 64.		

5C CHAI WAN LOOP (POTTINGER PEAK COUNTRY TRAIL) OR CHAI WAN
BIG WAVE BAY 🅚 🅡 🆂🅲

A pleasant walk with only one really scenic spot — but one that is worth i
taking in views of Shek O and Lei Yue Mun. This hike may be most useful as
alternative access to Dragon's Back, Hike 5B. There are also paths to the shore along
way, or you can break off the trail and go to Big Wave Bay. A shorter version is a
pleasant, either starting at the top of Shek O Peninsula or at Big Wave Bay, wh
entails more climbing.

Distance: 4.8 km/3 mi	Difficulty: 2/5	Time: 1 hr 30 min
Rise: 312 m	Map 5	
Countryside Map Grid: • Start: 14–15 and 65–66 • Finish: 16–17 and 62–63		

LEI YUE MUN–SAI WAN FORT MORNING WALK 🄳 🄺 🄽 🄡 🄢

Not far from Tai Tam Gap, Lei Yue Mun Park and Village nestles above Shau Kei
n, on the site of an old British Army base, the Sai Wan Fort. The Morning Walk
anders up the hill behind the park and surprises the visitor with close-up views of
shipping channel. When you're feeling adventurous and want to explore an out-of-
-way part of Hong Kong, try this hike.

Distance: 1 km/0.6 mi	Difficulty: 2/5	Time: 30 min
Rise: 80 m	Map 5	
Countryside Map Grid: 15 and 66		

Hub Amenities

·re are many restaurants and snack shops in Shek O; a favorite is the Chinese Thai
taurant just beyond the bus stop. They are used to hikers and keep the beer cold.
·re are toilets at the beach. In Big Wave Bay, there is a snack bar and also toilets. If
finish up at Tai Tam Gap (Shek O Roundabout), you can opt for the many facilities
Chai Wan or Stanley. Chai Wan has snack shops and bakeries at the MTR station,
Stanley has restaurants, bars and grocery stores.

N

– – – – –	5A
– · – · –	5B
· · · · · ·	5C
─────	5D

Chai Wan Road

Shing Tai Road

Chai Wan

Siu Sai Wan

Chai Wan Road

Cape Collinson Road

Lin Shing Road

Tai Tam Gap Correctional Institution

HIKE 5C alternative

Tai Tam Gap

Pottinger Peak
▲ 312

HIKE 5B alternative

Pottinger Gap (Ma Tong Au)

Tai Tam Road

Shek O Road

HIKE 4A (HKT 6)

▲ 348 Mount Collinson

HIKE 5B alternative

HKT 8

Shek O Road

Big Wave Bay Beach

HKT 7

Big Wave Bay (Tai Long Wan)

Tai Tam Road

Shek O Road

Tai Tam Harbor

Dragon's Back

Big Wave Bay Road

HIKE 5B BIKE TRAIL

▲ 284 Shek O Peak

Red Hill Peninsula

Shek O Wan

Shek O Village

Shek O Road

Shek O Country Park

Shek O Beach

Tai Tam Bay

To Tei Wan Village

D'Aguilar Peninsula

A HONG KONG TRAIL SECTION 7 — TAI TAM ROAD TO TO TEI WAN **P R S X**

long but easy walk, this trail has a dull start but finishes
h beautiful coastal views and glimpses of seaside
ages. This is a good path for a run. Beware, though,
at the end of the trail, you have only three ways out:
up, up about 700 stairs, back the way you came, or by
cking a boat to Tai Tam.

> Distance: 7.5 km/4.7 mi
> Difficulty: 1/5 but the stairs at the end are 5/5
> Time: 2 hr
> Rise: 250 m
> Maps 4 and 5
> Countryside Map Grid:
> • Start: 13–14 and 63
> • Finish: 15–16 and 60–61

To Get There

trailhead is on Tai Tam Road.

Bus:

Traveling towards Chai Wan: get off the bus just after it crosses the Tai Tam Reservoir Dam.

Traveling towards Stanley: As you come from Chai Wan, watch out the left side as you come down a hill and when you see the dam ahead on the left, ask the driver to stop.

Car:

ere is no parking, although people do pull their cars in at the trailhead.

Foot:

ng Kong Trail Section 6; see Hike 4A

m Tai Tam Reservoir Road; see end of Hike 3D

ere is a weekend ferry between Stanley and the "Hobie Cat Beach" (nicknamed for its ularity with sailboat enthusiasts) at To Tei Wan.

e trail is marked by a map board on the north side of Tai Tam Road, at the end of ng Kong Trail Section 6, Hike 4A; the trail runs down to the south.

Steps and a ramp lead down to the reservoir catchwater. Walk along the catchwater t some movable dams, then cross the catchwater and follow it along the far side to left. You will see a wooden Hong Kong Trail marker. The next 2.5 km/1.6 mi is a asant but unremarkable paved path with limited views. The path is shaded and can slippery. We have seen wild dogs about (see "What You Should Know").

151

At marker H070, the trail forks: stay right — the left fork is a dead end. Cros: dam/bridge with a nice waterfall just before marker H071.

Well past marker H073, you will find two park benches, rather an odd placem as there is no view and you really shouldn't need a rest yet. Then at marker H074, path opens up to magnificent views of Tai Tam Harbor, Red Hill Peninsula, Stanley a the shipping channel. The trail retreats to the woods for the next 500 meters or so, the views will be back shortly.

Cross a gorge with a pretty waterfall at marker H077, then look down for a glim of a village with gardens and a bright yellow temple. Footpaths lead down to the villa The trail winds back into the wooded area, passing more paths going down to villa and up to Shek O Road and another wooden Hong Kong Trail marker.

Near marker H079 there is an **emergency telephone**.

There are more views of Red Hill Peninsula and Stanley behind it at marker HG then the trail forks: take the left fork. Soon, you can hear the sounds of machinery the quarry ahead of you.

The trail seems to end at marker H083 as you go down a dirt path through la shrubs. Turn left at the Hong Kong Trail marker and then go down stone and dirt sta You will reach an intersection with a path coming down from your left, and a signpc

- **Shek O Peak (Hong Kong Trail Section 8) — 1.5 km/0.9 mi; 1 hr — left**
- Tai Tam Road — 6.75 km/4.2 mi; 2 hr — back

Ahead of you is the Hobie Cat Beach at To Tei Wan. The trail continues up to left, but take some time to go down to the Nam Kee Store on the beach for a look at view and a drink or snack before you tackle the stairs. The people at Nam Kee may a find you a boat ride to Stanley for a small fee.

When ready, go back to the signpost and climb the 700 stairs to Shek O Ro passing H084 about 550 steps up.

 ## To Continue to Hike

- Go up the Dragon's Back — Hike 5B

 ## To Leave the Trail

At Shek O Road, you can catch the No. 9 bus (and on weekends the No. 309) back Tai Tam Road, or down to Shek O Village. Shek O and Big Wave Bay are fun to explc they have a real village feel. At Big Wave Beach, you can walk out along the cliff to the ancient rock carvings — no one seems to have a clue when or why they were ma but they are old.

B HONG KONG TRAIL SECTION 8 (DRAGON'S BACK) — TO TEI WAN TO BIG WAVE BAY

nown as "Dragon's Back," the trail traces the ridge lines
 series of rises on top of Shek O Peak (284 m). The
 nning views of both sides of Shek O Peninsula, with
 ·y mansions, a golf course, beach villages, para-gliders,
 ·s, and islands in the distance, make this one of Hong
 ·g's most popular walks. The trail divides into three
 ·ions: first, the climb up to and along the ridge of the
 ·gon's Back; next, very flat sections through the trees
 along a paved road; last, down through the trees to
 Wave Bay (Tai Long Wan). The trail can be made
 ·rter and easier by accessing it at different points, as
 ·ed under "Alternatives" below.

Distance: 8.5 km/5.3 mi
Difficulty: 4/5
Time: 2 hr 30 min
Rise: 312 m
Map 5
Countryside Map Grid:
Start: 15–16 and 60–61
Finish: 16–17 at 62–63
The trail travels north to a U-turn at 14–15 and 64.

To Get There

Bus:

Bus No. 9 from Shau Kei Wan to To Tei Wan

Minibus No. 16M from Stanley to the Shek O roundabout and catch bus No. 9 to
To Tei Wan.

Car:

·re are a few parking spots near To Tei Wan.

, best to ask the bus driver to let you off at To Tei Wan. You can also look for several
·dmarks: the stop is immediately after a little park and a small parking lot, both on
· right side of the road; as you look west toward the Stanley area, the stop is across
·n the end of Red Hill Peninsula. If you pass the quarry, you have gone too far.

Hop off the bus at a map board, an **emergency phone**, and a small canopy with a
· for a cycling trail. The path leads up stone stairs to the left of the map board.

Soon after, a little side path off to the right leads to an abandoned homestead.
·re are overgrown banana trees and remnants of farm buildings.

Return to the trail up a combination of steep stairs and dirt path to the next marker;
·sure to turn around for views of Chung Hom Kok, Stanley Peninsula, and Tai Tam
·bor, as well as the Tai Tam Reservoirs to the north, with Parkview in the distance.

At marker H085, a side trail goes left to a covered pavilion and picnic area; the
·n path continues straight up a dirt path to a series of steep stairs interspersed with

a flat, rocky dirt section. At the top of the last set of stairs, there is a signpost point left (the right is marked as dangerous and off-limits). Stay on the main trail (left) becomes flat and mostly dirt, leading to a JUNCTION:

- **Shek O Peak — ahead (no distance noted but it is a scant kilometer to peak [about 0.5 mi] and about 200 meters to the ridge)**
- Tai Tam Gap — 3.5 km/2.2 mi; 1 hr 30 min — left. A flat cycling trail reconne with the main trail as it heads down from the Dragon's Back.
- Shek O Road — 0.5 km/0.3 mi; 15 min — back

When you reach the top of the ridge: wow! Take advantage of the bench here soak up the views of Shek O Village, the beaches and the views to the south. A l path to the right leads to another viewing spot. Not content with views below? weekends, look up and you are likely to see paragliders riding the air currents.

Head left along the top of the ridge, up Shek O Peak (284 m) and along the Drag Back, as it rolls up and down along several rises; the trail will alternate between flat steep, rocky and smooth, protected by shrubs and extremely exposed. Then you concrete marker H087 and a JUNCTION:

- **Tai Tam Gap — 2.5 km/1.6 mi; 1 hr — ahead**
- To Tei Wan — 1.5km/1 mi; 30 min — back (despite the sign, the distance i Shek O Road, not to Tei Wan Village)

Well-positioned rocks provide seats for you to take in the views to the south of Wave Bay and the Cape Collinson Correctional Institution. If you're lucky, you hear the band practicing.

At marker H088, a bench provides a nice respite; the views are stupendous! Scram up one last small peak, then down one last steep hill to reach marker H089, when post directs you to the left. Proceed down the rocky, rutted path along some stairs into the dirt. You arrive abruptly at a flat path and a JUNCTION:

- **Tai Tam Gap — 2 km/1.25 mi; 1 hr — right**
- Shek O Road — 2 km/1.25 mi; 1 hr — left (the bike trail)
- Hong Kong Trail (no distance noted but it's about 2.5 km/1.6 mi; 1 hr) — bac

You will now enter a heavily wooded, tree-covered area that has few views; the t is flat, punctuated by several rocks crossing streambeds, and many tree roots lying wait to grab your toes! Pass markers H090 through H093. Continue on this flat path until you come to an open area with a water tank on your left. Go down concrete road a short way to a JUNCTION:

- **Big Wave Bay — 2.5 km/1.6 mi; 1 hr — right**
- Tai Tam Gap — 0.2 km/0.1 mi; 5 min — left
- Shek O Peak — 2.5 km/1.6 mi; 1 hr 15 min — back

You are faced with some CHOICES:

- **To continue the hike, go right along the paved road. The road curves around Mount Collinson (348 m), giving you views of the huge cemeteries at Shau Kei Wan (Buddhist, Muslim, Sai Wan War, Roman Catholic, and Chinese) as well as the godowns of Chai Wan.**

- To exit, turn left a short distance along the road as it curves down to a gate. Go around the gate, passing the Tai Tam Gap Correctional Institution on your right, to Shek O Road. See Countryside Map Grid 14–15 and 63–64. Turn right on Shek O Road. There is a bus stop just a short distance on the left hand side of the road. You need to walk out to the roundabout to wave down a minibus to Stanley or Chai Wan, or just catch the first taxi you see.

- Walk to Chai Wan; see Hike 5C.

The road around Mount Collinson ends at Pottinger Gap (Ma Tong Au), a clearing with a shelter and some BBQ tables. Cross the clearing to the catchwater and follow it to the right, to a set of steps at the Hong Kong Trail marker. These steps go steadily downhill through woods with occasional views. You emerge at the edge of Big Wave Bay Village. Congratulate yourself as you pass marker H100.

To Leave the Trail

For an interesting detour, go to Big Wave Bay Beach and check out the primitive rock carving. To go to Shek O Village, wind downhill through the village, crossing a canal, then veer to the right, away from the beach, to the parking lot. Cross the parking lot to get to the road, and at the roundabout, turn left past the golf course to Shek O Village.

Alternatives

You can do the trail in reverse, starting at Big Wave Bay. To find the trail, go to the seaward end of the parking lot at Big Wave Bay and walk down the paved road, past the shops. At the intersection, go left over the bridge (do not go to the beach), then uphill through the village. You will pass the post office. Eventually the lane you are climbing becomes a path and then leads to uphill stairs, with the Hong Kong Trail marker H100 at the foot of the stairs. When you reach the catchwater at the top of the stairs, go left to a grassy field, then straight along the road on the far side of the field.

Note: *Parking at Big Wave Bay is now metered, with a two-hour maximum. As of this writing, there were no meters at Shek O, so you could park there and walk up to Big Wave Bay. The trail in reverse deposits you on Shek O Road, at a bus stop. If you want a taxi, you will have to call one.*

2. For a more scenic alternative when taking the trail from Big Wave Bay (see above), cross Big Wave Bay Beach and take the 1100-plus steps up Pottinger Peak (312 m); see Hike 5C in reverse; Countryside Map Grid 16–17 and 63–64. At the end of the steps, there is a clearing with trees and benches. At the far end, a sign indicates:

- **Pottinger Gap (Ma Tong Au) — 1 km/0.6 mi; 20 min — left**
- Cape Collinson — 1 km/0.6 mi; 30 min — right; see Hike 5C.
- Big Wave Bay — 1 km/0.6 mi; 40 min — back

Follow the catchwater to Pottinger Gap, there meeting Hong Kong Trail Section 8.

3. For a shorter hike, pick up the trail at the Tai Tam Gap Correctional Institution; at the Shek O Roundabout, walk down Shek O Road, to either the Correctional Institute driveway or stairs alongside it, on the left. Continue to the right up to a map board. Then hike the trail reverse, ending in To Tei Wan.

4. For another variation, access the hike from Chai Wan; see Hike 5C.

5C CHAI WAN LOOP (POTTINGER PEAK COUNTRY TRAIL) OR CHAI WAN TO BIG WAVE BAY

his route provides an alternative access to the Dragon's
ck (Hike 5B) and a pleasant loop on its own for a change
pace. Its scenic moments are few but impressive. You
ay choose to return to Chai Wan on the Pottinger Peak
untry Trail or stop off at Big Wave Bay. For a longer
ting, combine the hike with a visit to the Hong Kong
useum of Coastal Defense in Shau Kei Wan. The trail is
ood choice for a run. For a shorter trip with more views
r stride, you can begin at the Shek O Roundabout or at
, Wave Bay. See details below.

> Distance: 4.8 km/3 mi
> Difficulty: 2/5
> Timing: 1 hr 30 min
> Rise: 312 m
> Map 5
> Countryside Map Grid:
> • Start: 14–15 and 65–66
> • Finish: 16–17 and 63–64
> • Big Wave Bay is at
>   16–17 and 62–63

To Get There

u begin the trail in Chai Wan.

MTR:

ke the MTR to Chai Wan, Exit E, and cross the road on the overpass, then head uphill
Chai Wan Road.

Bus:

ses No. 8, 81A, and 82, among others, run to Chai Wan Road from Central; get off at
Chai Wan Road stop.

the Chai Wan Road bus stop you will see stairs going up to the left. These lead to the
ng Wah Housing Estate. At the top of the steps, turn right and walk up the hill to a
s stop, guardhouse, and taxi stand. Passing the guard house, climb up the road to Tai
m Road. (If you prefer, you can access Tai Tam Road from Chai Wan Road.) Turn left
ng Tai Tam Road. Across the road you will see a large slope with a guardrailed trail
ng the top, descending to the road in steps. Shortly after passing this landmark (about
e tenth of a mile from where you emerged on Tai Tam Road), on the left, a paved path
scends slightly downward. At the time we took it, it was marked by a blue guardrail.
e trail follows a catchwater, and it is rather trash-strewn but wide enough to run.

Cross a paved reservoir service road and walk along the catchwater. The trail is
ed by local residents and is dotted with little huts containing decrepit exercise bikes
d home-brewed refreshments. There are occasional views of the water channel and
cemeteries on Pottinger Peak (312 m).

Cross a cement bridge over a very pretty gorge — we heard lots of dogs at a hou in the gorge but they did not approach the trail — and go left to stay on the catchwat When you reach a paved road, go right and climb the hill to Tai Tam Road, just befc the roundabout to Shek O and Tai Tam.

Go left on Tai Tam Road and left again at the roundabout, towards the Tai Tam G Correctional Institution. (You can begin the trail at this point if you prefer a short walk.)

Ascend the road towards the Correctional Institution and turn right at the fi intersection. Climb the hill to a signboard, and you have some CHOICES:

- **left along the road**
- Dragon's Back, — right; see Hike 5B.

You will have a few views of Chai Wan but will mostly follow along a wooded ro: passing H094. Eventually, the road will end in Ma Tong Au (Pottinger Gap), a cleari with a picnic area and a signboard. Pick up the catchwater in the direction you w: going, towards the Hong Kong Trail marker. Ignore the marker and stay on t catchwater. You are now on the Pottinger Peak Country Trail.

The trail will show you a view of the Shek O headland, Big Wave Bay and Tso T Wan. At a clearing, there is a JUNCTION:

- **Cape Collinson — 1 km/0.6 mi; 30 min — ahead (but the road is actua 1.9 km/1.1 mi ahead).**
- Big Wave Bay — 1 km/0.6 mi; 40 min — right
- Pottinger Gap (Ma Tong Au) — 1 km/0.6 mi; 20 min — back

Next, you come to a marker:

- **Cape Collinson Road — 0.8 km/0.5 mi; 20 min — ahead (see above)**
- Pottinger Gap (Ma Tong Au) — 1.1 km/0.7 mi; 45 min — back

There is also a marker with an arrow pointing you to steps up — a short way there is a little shed which seems to be a gardener's hut or possibly a camp site. Contin past marker C4201 to a path on the right to a lookout point and pavilion. On the left marker indicates the path ahead:

- **Cape Collinson Road — 0.3 km/0.2 mi; 15 min**

Pass the marker and begin down a series of steps towards Chai Wan to arrive Cape Collinson Road, where there is another marker:

- **Chai Wan via Cape Collinson Road — 2 km/1.25 mi; 1 hr 45 min — ahead**
- Ma Tong Au (Pottinger Gap) — 1.9 km/1.2 mi; 1 hr 30 min — back

Go left along the road. A path leads to the shore (Cape Collinson) and a road to the Cape Collinson Correctional Institution. The road is accessible to cars.

CHOICES:

- Follow stairs down to the housing estates and into Chai Wan
- Continue along Cape Collinson Road to return to your starting point.

To Begin the Hike at Big Wave Bay

- To find the trail, go to the seaward end of the parking lot at Big Wave Bay and walk down the paved road, past the shops. At the intersection, go left over the bridge (do not go to the beach), then uphill through the village. You will pass the post office. Eventually the lane you are climbing becomes a path and then leads to uphill stairs, with the Hong Kong Trail marker H100 at the foot of the stairs. When you reach the top of the stairs, turn left on the catchwater. At Pottinger Gap (Ma Tong Au), go right.

- For a more scenic alternative when beginning at Big Wave Bay, cross Big Wave Bau Beach and take the 1100-plus steps up Pottinger Peak (312 m); see Hike 5C in reverse; and see Countryside Map Grid 16–17 and 63–64. At the end of the steps, there is a clearing with trees and benches.

    At the far end, a sign indicates:

- **Cape Collinson — 1 km/0.6 mi; right**
- Pottinger Gap (Ma Tong Au) — 1 km/0.6 mi; 20 min — left
- Big Wave Bay — 1 km/0.6 mi; 40 min — back

5D LEI YUE MUN – SAI WAN FORT MORNING WALK

Ⓓ Ⓚ Ⓝ Ⓡ Ⓧ

Agently climbing, little-known trail, this walk ends up at the Sai Wan Fort. The views of Lei Yue Mun Channel, the narrow entrance to the harbor, are unique and splendid. It's a good walk for kids, and you could combine it with a visit to the Coastal Defense Museum in Shau Kei Wan.

Distance: 1 km/0.6 mi
Difficulty: 2/5
Time: 30 min
Rise: 80 m
Ⓝ Map 5
Countryside Map Grid: 15 and 66

To Get There

On Foot:
From the Shau Kei Wan MTR stop take the exit to Shau Kei Wan Main Street. Follow th[e] sign to McDonald's. The temple on the left is worth a look. Walk along Factory Stre[et] towards the HSBC sign to Chai Wan Road, and left uphill along Chai Wan Road. Ne[ar] the top of the hill you will see the large green sign: "Lei Yue Mun Holiday Village."

By Bus:
Bus No. 9 from Exit A at the Shau Kei Wan MTR Station

By Car:
There is no parking that we know of at Lei Yue Mun Village. There are parking lots [in] Shau Kei Wan, but the most convenient lot may be at No. 200 Tai Tam Road, up the h[ill] from the village. From Chai Wan Road, go right at the turn marked Shek O.

Turn left at a green sign up a paved road, behind St. Basil's School and some apartme[nt] buildings. As you crest the hill, look to the right for a sign for the Sai Wan Fort Morni[ng] Walk. The old army barracks have been restored as holiday villas and administrat[ive] offices. One shows a date of 1936.

The trail follows along the road, with an unfortunate chain-link fence on the rig[ht] but some entertaining views of Chai Wan on the left. There are detour paths to the le[ft,] and if they are not too overgrown you can clamber up for a view of the Lei Yue M[un] Channel. The paths rejoin the road on the other side of the hill.

Continuing up the road, you will find a series of earthen stairs with wood rise[rs]

CHOICES:

- Take the stairs up hill, passing little hobby garden plots as you go, to a trigonometric station and the old fort at the top. Follow the path around the fort and take stairs down a bit. There is a superb view and a sign showing distances to various international cities, as well as some abandoned bunkers and what looks like a former BBQ area. There is also an **emergency phone**.
- Stay on the road, which wends its way to the old fort.

Now retrace your steps back down to the start.

Note: *The village is open to the public but you must have a reservation to stay there and use the facilities. It has quite extensive recreational facilities, including a riding stable.*

APPENDICES

Extended Hikes

Hong Kong Trail in its entirety:

Hikes 1A, 1K, 1L, 2F, 3A, 4A, 5A, 5B

Wan Chai Loop:

Wan Chai Gap (Hub 2) to Black's Link to Wong Nai Chung Road, Hike 2D; and Lady Clementi's Ride, Hike 2E (Yellow Walk), and Hike 3H; then Hong Kong Trail Sections 4 and 3, Hikes 2C, 1L, and 2F

The Peak to Big Wave Bay shortcut:

Hong Trail Sections 1–4 to Parkview, Hikes 1A, 1K, 1L, and 2F; then Tai Tam Reservoir Road, Hike 3D; to Hong Kong Trail 6–8, Hikes 4A, 5A and 5B

Stanley to Quarry Bay:

Wilson Trail Sections 1 and 2 (the Twins to Parkview to Quarry Bay), Hikes 3B and 3F in reverse

Stanley to Wan Chai or Central:

Wilson Trail Section 1 — the Twins to Parkview, Hike 3F in reverse; then to Bowen Road, Hike 2B; and from there either to the Central Green Trail, Hike 1G, or Wan Chai Green Trail, Hike 2A

South Bay to Parkview via Repulse Bay Gap:

See Hike 3D

Parkview to Big Wave Bay via Sir Cecil's Ride:

Sir Cecil's Ride, Hike 3C; to Mount Parker Road and then to Boa Vista, Hike 4B; and down to Big Wave Bay, Hike 5A and/or 5B

Chai Wan to Big Wave Bay:

Chai Wan, Hike 5C; to Shek O Roundabout to Dragon's Back, Hike 5B

Tai Tam to Stanley the long way:

Tai Tam Reservoir Road, Hike 3D; to Mount Parker Road to Sir Cecil's Ride, Hike 3C; to Parkview to Violet Hill and the Twins to Stanley, Hike 3F

Central to the Peak and Back:

Chatham Path, Hike 1G in reverse; to Barker Road to the Peak on Lloyd or Hospital Path, Hike 1H; to Old Peak Road back down, Hike 1F

Wan Chai to Tai Tam:

From Wan Chai Gap on Middle Gap Road, Hike 2D; to Hong Kong Trail Section 4, Hike 2F; to Black's Link, Hike 2C; to Tai Tam Reservoir Road, Hike 3D

Appendices

- The Peak to Wan Chai the long way:
    Hong Kong Trail Sections 1–3, Hikes 1A, 1K and 1L; to Lady Clementi's R
    Hike 2E (Yellow Walk); to Middle Gap Road, Hike 2D; to Black's Link, Hike
    to Bowen Road, Hike 2B; and then Wan Chai on the Green Trail, Hike 2A
- The Peak to Tai Tam Road:
    Hong Kong Trail Sections 1–6, Hikes 1A, 1K, 1L, 2F, 3A and 4A
- The Peak to Mount Davis:
    Morning Trail and Cheung Po Tsai Path, Hike 1B, or Pik Shan Path, Hike 1I
    Mount Davis, Hike 1N
- Killer Hike:
    Hong Kong Trail Section 5, Hike 3A; to Mount Parker Road, from there up
    Tam Reservoir Road to the Upper Path to Repulse Bay Gap, Hike 3D; then
    Twins, Hike 3F

II Fitness Hikes 🅕

1B The Morning Trail and Cheung Po Tsai Path — Harlech Road and Lung Fu S
    Fitness Trail.

1C The Loop — Harlech Road and Lugard Road (Pok Fu Lam Tree Walk)

1K Hong Kong Trail Section 2 — Pok Fu Lam Reservoir Road to Peel Rise — there
    a few stations between H015 and H016

2B Bowen Road

2E Aberdeen Country Park Hikes

3F Wong Nai Chung Reservoir Park Fitness Trail — Tai Tam Country Trail — a v
    short one!

4B Mount Parker Road — a few stations at Quarry Gap

III Disabled-Friendly Hikes 🅓

1B The Morning Trail

1C The Loop — Harlech Road and Lugard Road

1H Peak Loops

2B Bowen Road

2C Black's Link

2E Aberdeen Country Park Hikes — with P.H.A.B. BBQ site

3D Tai Tam Reservoir Road — not the loop

3J Repulse Bay Promenade — access from and return to Beach Road to avoid sta

4B Mount Parker Road

5D Lei Yue Mun–Sai Wan Fort Morning Walk

Kid-Friendly Hikes/Short Walks

The Morning Trail and Cheung Po Tsai Path

The Loop — Harlech Road and Lugard Road

Governor's Walk

Chatham Path and Central Green Trail

Peak Loops

Mount Davis Trail

Bowen Road

Black's Link

Aberdeen Country Park Hikes

Sir Cecil's Ride — but this is quite long, so consider doing only part of it

Lady Clementi's Ride

Repulse Bay Seaview Promenade

Chung Hom Kok

Hong Pak Country Trail

Quarry Bay Tree Walk

Chai Wan Loop (Pottinger Peak Country Trail) or Chai Wan to Big Wave Bay

Lei Yue Mun–Sai Wan Fort Morning Walk

Family Trails, Nature Walks, Tree Walks and Green Trails

The Morning Trail and Cheung Po Tsai Path

The Loop — Harlech Road and Lugard Road (Pok Fu Lam Tree Walk)

Central Green Trail

Pok Fu Lam Reservoir Family Walk (end of 1A)

Wan Chai Gap Road and Wan Chai Gap Green Trail

Aberdeen Country Park Hikes

Hong Kong Trail Section 4 — Wan Chai Gap to Wong Nai Chung Gap — at the beginning

Sir Cecil's Ride

Tai Tam Reservoir Country Park Loop

Tai Tam Country Trail

Lady Clementi's Ride

Tai Tam Tree Walk

Wong Nai Chung Tree Walk

Quarry Bay Tree Walk

Lei Yue Mun–Sai Wan Fort Morning Walk

Appendices

Repulse Bay Seaview Promenade

Chung Hom Kok

Stanley Fort

Hong Kong Trail Section 6 — in reverse

Mount Parker Road to Boa Vista Hill

Hong Kong Trail Section 7 — Tai Tam Road to To Tei Wan

Chai Wan Loop (Pottinger Peak Country Trail) or Chai Wan to Big Wave Bay

Lei Yue Mun–Sai Wan Fort Morning Walk

Scenic/Historical Hikes

Hong Kong Trail Section 1 — the Peak to Pok Fu Lam

The Morning Trail — Pinewood Battery Detour

The Loop — Harlech Road and Lugard Road

Governor's Walk

High West

Central Green Trail

Peak Loops

Hong Kong Trail Section 2 — Pok Fu Lam To Aberdeen

Peel Rise — the Peak to Aberdeen

Mount Davis Trail

Bowen Road

Black's Link

Aberdeen Country Park Hikes

Hong Kong Trail Section 4 — Wan Chai Gap to Wong Nai Chung Gap

Hong Kong Trail Section 5 (Mount Butler)— Wong Nai Chung Gap to Mount Parker Road

Wilson Trail Section 2 — Parkview to Quarry Bay

Sir Cecil's Ride

Tai Tam Reservoir Country Park Loop

Tai Tam Country Trail

Wilson Trail Section 1 — Violet Hill and the Twins

Repulse Bay Seaview Promenade

Chung Hom Kok

Stanley Fort

Mount Parker Road to Boa Vista Hill

Hong Pak Country Trail

Quarry Bay Tree Walk

Hong Kong Trail Section 7 — Tai Tam Road to To Tei Wan

Hong Kong Trail Section 8 (Dragon's Back) — To Tei Wan to Big Wave Bay

Appendices